CONTENTS

THE STORECUPBOARD

Oriental food is now so popular that it is increasingly easy to buy the ingredients that give an intriguing exotic flavour.

Of course, not everyone lives within reach of a Chinese or Japanese shop, but a well-stocked supermarket should be able to supply

most of the ingredients used in this book. Health food shops are another good source of nuts, seeds and Japanese ingredients.

Flavourings: coconut milk, very rich, sold in cans or as a powder; dried bonito (tuna) flakes, widely used in Japanese cooking; dried shrimps, usually soaked before use, pinker ones are generally fresher; kamaboko (also spelled namaboko) and naruto, dried Japanese fishcake; mirin, Japanese sweetened rice wine; miso, soya bean paste with a wonderful deep flavour; red curry paste, hot Thai flavouring sold in jars or plastic packets; rice wine, Chinese shaoxing and Japanese sake are very different, but dry sherry can be used instead; shrimp paste (also known as blachan, various spellings), made from salted, fermented shrimps, is used sparingly to add a pungent, savoury flavour – keep it well-wrapped in the refrigerator; wasabi, Japanese horseradish, is less hot and pungent than Western horseradish, sold as a powder or paste.

Tamarind is an acidic fruit, widely used in Asian cooking to give a refreshing, sour taste. It is sold as a ready-to-use paste or dried in blocks. To extract tamarind juice from dried tamarind pulp, mix 2 tbsp pulp with 4 tbsp water and push the mixture through a sieve. For a stronger flavour, leave to soak for 1–2 hours before sieving.

Herbs and spices: basil, always used fresh (red basil has a more subtle flavour than green basil); chillies, used fresh or dried, whole or in flakes; coriander – bunches of fresh leaves and stalks have a very different flavour from the round brown seeds; galangal – looks similar to ginger and has a subtle flavour; garlic; garlic chives, which look like large chives, but have a garlic flavour; kaffir lime leaves have a citrus aroma, available dried or fresh (keep fresh leaves in the freezer); lemon grass has a subtle lemony flavour (fresh is far superior to dried; remove the tough outer leaves and use the tender core); root ginger – buy fresh, firm, smooth knobs of ginger – usually peeled, then grated, sliced or shredded; peppercorns – black, white, green, and the reddish-brown Sichuan peppercorns (also known as aromatic pepper) all have different flavours; seven-pepper spice, or Japanese pepper, is a blend of spices, including chillies, sesame, white pepper, nori and dried orange peel; lemon pepper can be used instead of seven-pepper spice; onion pepper is another aromatic spice blend; star anise is a beautiful star-shaped seed pod with a distinctive and aromatic flavour – use whole or extract the seeds; turmeric, usually bought as a powder, adds a bright yellow colour and slightly bitter flavour which is often used to balance sweetness.

Nuts and seeds: these add a crunchy texture to stir-fries, and are sometimes served separately, as garnishes – cashew nuts, natural (unsalted) peanuts, sesame seeds, sunflower seeds.

Oils and vinegars: chilli oil is used as a flavouring; groundnut or peanut oil has a neutral flavour and is very good for the high temperatures needed for deep-frying; sesame oil has a rich, strong, nutty taste, and can be used – sparingly – for frying or as a flavouring; sunflower oil is an excellent all-purpose cooking oil.

Wine vinegar and garlic vinegar have a place in the Oriental kitchen, but most common is rice vinegar, made from fermented rice. Cider vinegar can be used in place of white rice vinegar. Chinese black rice vinegar has a rich taste, somewhat like balsamic vinegar.

Pickles: pickled Chinese cabbage and pickled radish are often used in stir-fries; pickled ginger is sold sliced or shredded – the shredded version is pink, and is most often used as a garnish.

Sauces: bean sauce or paste is a thick, salty, aromatic condiment made from soya beans; it may be black or yellow. Fish sauce (called *nam pla* in Thailand and *nuoc mam* in Vietnam), made from salted and fermented fish, is a very pungent clear brown liquid; it loses a lot of its 'punch' and fishiness when heated. Hoisin sauce is a dark brown, sweet and spicy sauce made from soya beans. Oyster sauce is thick, rich and savoury. Soy sauce varies from country to country: China has light and dark versions, both saltier than the Japanese; *kecap manis* is darker, sweeter, Indonesian soy sauce.

Sea vegetables: sold dried and usually used as flavourings or garnishes. They can be reconstituted very quickly in water. Hijiki, black, sold in pieces; konbu (also spelled kombu), similar to kelp, used to make dashi broth; nori, similar to laver, sold in paper-thin, purplish-black sheets – often toasted and then flaked; wakame, dark green. Dashi broth is widely available in instant form.

Vegetables (canned and dried): usually used for their texture. Bamboo shoots are pale yellow and crunchy; Chinese dried mushrooms have an intense flavour and chewy texture – to reconstitute, soak in warm water for about 20 minutes or until soft, then drain and squeeze dry, discard the hard stalks and use only the caps; straw mushrooms have a very mild flavour and soft texture, sold in cans; water chestnuts are white and very crisp, usually sold peeled in cans.

TYPES OF NOODLES

In almost all of the recipes in this book, the noodles are interchangeable, and you can use whichever is your favourite type. If you see any Japanese noodles that seem to be outrageously priced, they are probably te'uchi, *or hand-made.*

Beancurd noodles *(also called transparent noodles, cellophane noodles)*: fine vermicelli noodles. These always come tied in a bundle – either a large bundle, or a smaller bundle for one portion. The packets are marked 'beanthread', 'peastarch' or 'beanstarch'. Because of the processes used to make them, it is very difficult to separate the noodles when they are dry, which is why they are often sold in single-portion bundles. If the noodles are to be used to make a stuffing, they will have to be broken up after cooking. Beancurd noodles have a beautiful translucence to them once cooked, and they do not stick together, so they are useful in stir-fries and salads.

Chinese wheat noodles *(ho fen)*: flat, stick-like noodles. These have a heavy texture, and are great with vegetarian dishes or dishes with a lot of sauce. Flat rice noodles can be used if ho fen noodles are unavailable.

Chow mein noodles: thin, flat egg noodles. These are designed to hold chow mein sauce. Medium egg noodles can be used instead.

Egg noodles: made from wheatflour, egg and water, available in thread (fine) thickness or medium thickness.. These noodles are readily available and very popular. Egg noodles do not stick when stir-frying, are satisfying as an accompaniment, and absorb dressings easily, all of which makes them versatile and easy to work with. They can also be deep-fried very successfully.

Mie noodles: nests of Chinese egg noodles, made to a slightly less rich recipe. They are also available with chilli flavouring.

Ramen noodles: crinkly Japanese noodles, available fresh or dried. They are commonly sold as instant meals, with a flavoured soup base sachet in the pack with the noodles. They are very cheap, so just discard the flavour sachet and use the noodles. Ramen noodles are most often used in a soup-stew, a nutritious and filling one-pot meal.

Rice noodles: Chinese noodles made from rice flour and water, available in vermicelli, thread (fine) thickness, or flat (when they are sometimes called rice sticks). These are recognizable by their white colour and translucence, both when raw and cooked. They are easily confused with beancurd noodles, so look for the word 'rice' or 'riz' on the packet. Rice noodles have a bland flavour, which makes them ideal as an accompaniment for highly flavoured or rich dishes. Thread or fine rice noodles are ideal chopped and used as a stuffing or in a stir-fry. All rice noodles are great deep-fried.

Soba noodles: Japanese thin noodles, made from varying percentages of buckwheat flour. The more buckwheat they contain, the better they are (and the more expensive). Noodles with a buckwheat content of 40% are a good choice, and reasonably priced. They may be brown or green, so they will add a bit of colour to a salad or stir-fry. Soba noodles are quite filling, and are usually served in smaller portions than other noodles.

Somen noodles: Japanese, thin, very fine, wheatflour noodles. These are used for stir-fries, in soup and as an accompaniment. They are also sold in rainbow colours to use in a salad, which looks most attractive in the serving dish. They can be used as a substitute for udon noodles.

Udon noodles: Japanese, very narrow, ribbon-like, wheatflour noodles, available fresh or dried. The dried version is slightly flatter. These noodles have a satisfying texture and chewability. Udon noodles are excellent stir-fried, or used to make a satisfying soup-stew.

COOKING NOODLES SUCCESSFULLY

When cooking noodles, bear in mind what they will be used for. Noodles that will be in a soupy dish need to be slightly undercooked so they do not fall apart, whereas noodles that are to be stir-fried should be cooked in plenty of boiling water, in order to disperse the starch content. (It is the starch in the noodles that makes them stick together in cooking.)

Cook noodles as soon as possible before they are to be served. This is especially important for flat rice noodles which often stick.

There are basically two ways to cook noodles. The first is suitable for particularly fine noodles, such as beancurd noodles, rice vermicelli or egg thread noodles, as well as for nest noodles so that they keep their shape. Put the noodles into a very large basin and pour on plenty of boiling water, then leave to stand for the time suggested on the packet. Drain in a colander before using.

The second method, which should be used for larger dried noodles, is to plunge the noodles into a large pan of boiling water (use the biggest pan available, as you cannot have too much water to cook noodles). When a white foam – which is the starch from the noodles – rises to the surface, add a cup of cold water to the pan. When the water returns to the boil, add another cup of cold water. Some noodles will be cooked when the water boils for the third time, while others will need one more addition of cold water. The cold water ensures that the surface of the noodle does not break up and become 'furry', giving out more starch and spoiling your recipe. Drain and rinse the noodles before using.

NOODLES TO START

Fragrant noodle soups are a feature of many Asian cuisines, either as a delicate first course or as a sustaining snack at any time of day. Other starters use noodles in ingenious ways – as a stuffing for artichokes, a filling for spring rolls or as the base for crabcakes. All recipes serve 4–6 unless indicated otherwise.

HOT AND SOUR SOUP

This soup is sold on street corners all over Southeast Asia by mobile food vendors. They carry with them everything they need to make their particular speciality – wok, burner, ingredients – balanced in panniers across their shoulders. The soup is whipped up in a flash, and it is up to the customer to say how much chilli he wants in his dish.

200g/7oz egg thread noodles
1 tbsp sunflower oil
90g/3oz shiitake mushrooms, sliced

2 tbsp chopped fresh coriander
salt
115g/4oz watercress

FOR THE STOCK
1 tbsp tamarind pulp
2 dried red chillies
2 kaffir lime leaves
2.5cm/1in piece root ginger, chopped

5cm/2in piece galangal, chopped
1 stalk lemon grass, chopped
1 onion, quartered
1 litre/1³/4 pints water

TO GARNISH
1 fresh red chilli, thinly sliced
lime wedges

beansprouts

Put all the ingredients for the stock into a saucepan and bring to the boil. Simmer for 5 minutes. Strain.

Return the stock to the saucepan and bring back to the boil. Add the noodles and cook for 3 minutes. Using tongs or a slotted spoon, remove the noodles from the broth and divide among the serving bowls. Reserve the broth.

Heat the oil in a wok or large frying pan and cook the sliced mushrooms over a high heat for 1 minute or until they have softened. Add the broth and stir in the coriander. Add salt to taste.

Divide the watercress among the serving bowls and ladle the broth over the noodles and watercress. Garnish each bowl with a couple of red chilli slices, and serve hot, with lime wedges and beansprouts.

STUFFED LOTUS LEAVES

Lotus leaves and banana leaves can be found in most Oriental supermarkets. Using leaves as a wrapping keeps all the moisture and flavours in the stuffing, and the parcels look very exotic and impressive.

Makes 4 parcels

8 lotus leaves or banana leaves, washed
and cut into 20cm/8in squares
100g/3¹/2oz beancurd noodles
180g/6oz white fish fillet
1 tbsp red curry paste
3 shallots, finely chopped
3 spring onions, finely chopped
juice of 1 lime
1 tsp turmeric

¹/2 tsp crushed garlic
2 tsp fish sauce
1 tsp white peppercorns, crushed
2 fresh red chillies, seeded and chopped
100ml/3¹/2fl oz coconut milk
about 1 tbsp Indonesian soy sauce
(kecap manis), plus more for serving
1 egg, lightly beaten
chilli sauce, to serve

Soak the lotus leaves in warm water for about 10 minutes to soften. Blanch the lotus or banana leaves in boiling water for 6 minutes. Drain, refresh under cold running water and leave to drain.

Cook the noodles in plenty of boiling water for 3 minutes or according to packet instructions. Drain and snip them into pieces.

Put the fish fillet into a food processor and process until finely chopped. Alternatively, finely chop it by hand. Add the red curry paste, shallots, spring onions, lime juice, turmeric, crushed garlic, fish sauce, white pepper and red chillies. Process or mash until fairly smooth. Stir in the coconut milk. Season to taste with *kecap manis*, and stir in the egg and the noodles.

Lay out 4 of the lotus leaves, or banana leaves, on a work surface. Divide the fish stuffing among the leaves and fold the leaf neatly around the stuffing. If you are using banana leaves, you may find it easier to make a pleat in either side and fold in the edges, or wrap it like a present. Fold another leaf neatly around the first leaf to enclose completely. Secure with a wooden cocktail stick. Alternatively, place a strip of filling along the centre of a leaf, roll it up and secure both ends with cocktail sticks.

Steam the parcels over boiling water for 15–20 minutes, depending on their size. Serve immediately, piping hot, accompanied by chilli sauce and more Indonesian soy sauce.

Right: Hot and Sour Soup

SOUR SOUP WITH MEATBALLS

Here is a surprising but delicious combination: a light, piquant soup base with robust meatballs and rice vermicelli.

115g/4oz minced beef	1 tsp coriander seeds, crushed
115g/4oz minced pork	1 tsp black peppercorns, crushed
1 tbsp soy sauce	100g/3^1/$_2$oz rice vermicelli noodles
seeds from 1 star anise, crushed	chopped fresh coriander, to garnish

FOR THE STOCK

1 stalk lemon grass, lightly bruised	2.5cm/1in piece root ginger, chopped
1 onion, quartered	5cm/2in piece galangal, chopped
2 tbsp tamarind pulp	1 litre/1^3/$_4$ pints cold water
2 dried red chillies, chopped	

Mix together the minced beef and pork, soy sauce, star anise seeds, coriander seeds and black peppercorns, and shape into small balls. Refrigerate for at least 20 minutes.

Meanwhile, put all the ingredients for the stock into a large saucepan, bring to the boil and simmer for 10 minutes. Strain.

Return the stock to the saucepan and bring back to a gentle boil. Add the chilled meatballs and simmer for 10 minutes or until the meatballs are cooked. Add the rice vermicelli 2–3 minutes before the end of the cooking time. Serve hot, garnished with chopped coriander.

MARINATED DUCK ON A BED OF NOODLES

This recipe demonstrates how simply cooked noodles can be used as a foil for very rich ingredients.

3 tbsp medium or sweet sherry	salt and freshly ground black pepper
2 tbsp sunflower oil	350g/12oz duck breasts, skin removed
2 garlic cloves, crushed	200g/7oz flat rice noodles
5 seeds from a star anise, crushed	90g/3oz cucumber, cut into matchsticks
1 tbsp dark soft brown sugar	

Combine the sherry, 1 tablespoon of the oil, the garlic, star anise, brown sugar and seasoning in a shallow dish. Add the duck breasts and turn them so that they are well coated in the mixture. Leave the duck to marinate for at least 1 hour or, preferably, overnight.

Heat a heavy frying pan until it is very hot. Drain the duck breasts, reserving the marinade. Cook the duck in the hot pan over a high heat for 6–8 minutes on each side. At the end of this time, add the reserved marinade, plus a little water if necessary, and simmer to make a sauce with a coating consistency. Remove the duck breasts and set aside to cool. Spoon the sauce into a small serving dish.

Cook the noodles in plenty of boiling water for 5 minutes or according to packet instructions. Drain and rinse under cold running water. Drain well and toss with the remaining oil and the cucumber matchsticks.

Divide the noodles among the serving plates. Slice the cooled duck thinly, and arrange on top of the noodles. Serve with the sauce.

THAI SPRING ROLLS

Thai spring rolls are more subtle in flavour than the Chinese version. The filling here contains no meat, but you may like to add some cooked minced chicken or pork. These are ideal for parties, being only two-bite size.

Makes 32 spring rolls

2 tbsp plain flour	1 green pepper, finely chopped
150ml/5fl oz water	1 celery stick, finely chopped
80g/2^1/$_2$oz rice vermicelli noodles	2 spring onions, finely chopped
1 tbsp vegetable oil, plus more for	115g/4oz button mushrooms, finely chopped
deep-frying	2 tsp liquid seasoning, such as Maggi
1 garlic clove, crushed	8 spring roll sheets, 25cm/10in square

FOR THE DIPPING SAUCE

4 tbsp rice vinegar	^{1}/$_2$ tsp salt
4 tbsp caster sugar	1 small fresh red chilli, finely chopped

Mix the flour and water together in a small pan over a low heat, stirring constantly until thick and translucent. Pour into a small bowl and set aside.

Blanch the rice vermicelli in boiling water for 30 seconds, then drain well. Snip into 2.5cm/1in pieces and set aside in a large bowl.

Heat 1 tablespoon of the oil in a wok or large heavy frying pan over a high heat. Add the garlic, green pepper, celery, spring onions and button mushrooms and stir-fry until the vegetables are softened. Add the liquid seasoning. Use a slotted spoon to lift out the vegetables, and stir them into the rice vermicelli.

Divide each spring roll sheet into 4 squares. Place 2 teaspoons of the filling in the centre of each square. Fold three corners in and roll up to the fourth corner. Seal with a little of the flour and water paste.

To make the sauce, boil all the ingredients together, stirring constantly, until the sauce thickens, about 5 minutes. Leave to cool.

When you are ready to serve the spring rolls, heat oil in a wok or deep fat fryer until a light haze appears – about 180°C/350°F. Deep-fry the spring rolls in batches until they are golden brown all over. Drain on plenty of kitchen paper to ensure a crisp finish. Serve immediately, accompanied by the sauce.

FRAGRANT CHICKEN BROTH

A good, filling broth, and cheap to make too, but sophisticated enough to serve to guests for a light lunch or after-theatre supper.

1 chicken, weighing about 1.35kg/3lb	juice of 1 lime
1 litre/1³/4 pints water	2 small fresh red chillies, seeded and sliced
5cm/2in piece root ginger	3 tbsp chopped fresh coriander
2 onions, sliced	115g/4oz flat rice noodles
salt	2 spring onions, thinly sliced
2 tbsp fish sauce	shredded fresh red basil, to garnish
1 tsp black peppercorns	

Put the chicken in a large saucepan with the water, ginger, onions and a generous pinch of salt. Bring to the boil and simmer for 45 minutes.

Lift out the chicken, and cut all the meat from the bones. Slice the meat finely and set aside. Return the skin and bones to the saucepan, add the fish sauce and peppercorns and simmer for 2 hours, skimming occasionally. Strain the stock and add the lime juice, chillies and coriander. Keep warm.

Cook the noodles in boiling water for 5 minutes or according to packet instructions. Drain and divide among the serving bowls. Top with the sliced chicken and spring onions, ladle in the hot soup, garnish with shredded basil and serve immediately.

NABEYAKI UDON

This dish is unusual because of the eggs that are cooked in the broth.

60g/2oz shiitake mushrooms, sliced, or	8 thin slices kamaboko fishcake
30g/1oz dried Chinese mushrooms	4 eggs
1 sheet konbu	1 spring onion, finely chopped
1.5 litres/2¹/2 pints water	
1 tbsp miso paste	TO SERVE
400g/14oz udon noodles	dried bonito flakes
115g/4oz firm tofu, cut into cubes	chilli oil
90g/3oz French beans	soy sauce

If using dried mushrooms, soak them in warm water for 15 minutes; drain and remove the stalks. Soak the konbu in warm water for 15 minutes; drain and cut into strips.

Put the water and miso paste into a large saucepan – at least 3 litre/5 pint capacity – and bring to the boil. Add the noodles and return to a gentle boil, then add the tofu cubes and beans, the mushrooms, konbu and fishcake. Cover and simmer very gently for 5 minutes.

Carefully break the eggs into the simmering liquid, cover the pan and cook for a further 4–5 minutes.

Ladle into serving bowls and garnish with the spring onion. Serve immediately, accompanied by dried bonito flakes, chilli oil and soy sauce, to be added according to personal taste.

CHICKEN VERMICELLI SOUP

This really is a meal in itself – nutritious and full of flavour.

1 chicken, weighing about 1.35kg/3lb	salt and freshly ground black pepper
1 onion, quartered	2 litres/3¹/2 pints water
1 carrot, roughly chopped	90g/3oz egg thread noodles
1 leek, roughly chopped	15g/¹/2oz butter
2 celery sticks, roughly chopped	1 tbsp chopped fresh tarragon
1 tsp black peppercorns	
1 bouquet garni (bay, parsley, thyme	TO GARNISH
tied together in a bunch)	2 tbsp chopped fresh chives
	cayenne pepper

Cut the chicken breasts and legs from the body. Remove all the meat from the legs, as neatly as you can, and reserve the leg bones. Cut the chicken breast and leg meat into strips and set aside.

Preheat the oven to 200°C/400°F/Gas 6. Put the chicken carcass and leg bones in a roasting tin and cook in the oven for 45 minutes.

Transfer all the chicken bones and any cooking juices to a large saucepan. Add the onion, carrot, leek, celery, peppercorns, bouquet garni and a little salt. Pour in the water, bring to the boil and simmer for 1 hour. Strain the stock, taste and adjust the seasoning.

Break the noodles into small pieces (it is easiest to do this while they are still in the packet).

Heat the butter in a large saucepan, add the chicken strips and stir until cooked. Season well. Add the stock, the noodles and the tarragon. Simmer for 5 minutes, then serve hot, garnished with chives and cayenne pepper.

MUSHROOM AND GINGER BROTH

Dried Chinese mushrooms are very intense in flavour, and will satisfy anyone in this simple, quickly made soup.

15g/¹/2oz dried Chinese mushrooms	700ml/scant 1¹/4 pints hot vegetable stock
115g/4oz medium egg noodles	1 tsp mushroom ketchup
1 tbsp sunflower oil	1 tsp light soy sauce
2 garlic cloves, crushed	fresh coriander leaves, to garnish
2.5cm/1in piece root ginger, finely shredded	

Soak the Chinese mushrooms in 300ml/10fl oz hot water for 30 minutes. Drain, reserving the soaking water. Remove and discard the stalks, and slice the mushrom caps.

Soak the noodles in very hot water for 10 minutes.

Meanwhile, heat the oil in a wok or large open pan over a high heat. Add the garlic, ginger and sliced mushrooms. Stir-fry for 2 minutes.

Add the vegetable stock with the reserved mushroom soaking water and bring to the boil. Add the mushroom ketchup and soy sauce.

Drain the noodles and divide among the serving bowls. Ladle in the hot soup and serve immediately, garnished with coriander leaves.

Right: Mushroom and Ginger Broth

NOODLE-STUFFED ARTICHOKES

Make this in the spring when artichokes are cheap and abundant.

4 large globe artichokes	120ml/4fl oz single cream
juice of 1 lemon	salt and freshly ground black pepper
100g/3¹/₂oz soba noodles	4 quail's eggs
115g/4oz shelled fresh or frozen peas	cayenne pepper, to garnish
1 shallot, finely chopped	

Snap the stalk off each artichoke, pulling any tough stem fibres with it. Trim off any tough outer leaves. Cut straight across the top, about one-third of the way down, so that the choke is exposed. Use scissors to cut the tough points off the remaining outer leaves. Trim the base so it is flat. As each artichoke is prepared, drop it into a large bowl of water to which you have added the lemon juice. Cook the artichokes in boiling salted water for 15 minutes.

Meanwhile, cook the noodles in boiling water for 4 minutes or according to packet instructions. Drain and set aside.

Preheat the oven to 180°C/350°F/Gas 4. When the artichokes are cooked, remove them from the pan and drain upside down on kitchen paper. As soon as they are cool enough to handle, use a teaspoon to scoop out the chokes.

Divide the noodles among the artichokes, piling them in the central hollows. Top with the peas and shallot. Arrange the artichokes in a baking tin.

Season the cream well with salt and pepper. Pour the cream into the artichokes, nearly to the top. Break a quail's egg into the top of each one and sprinkle generously with cayenne pepper. Cover lightly with foil. Cook in the oven for 15 minutes. Serve piping hot.

NOODLE CRABCAKES

These cakes are most delicious made with fresh white crabmeat. However, you can substitute frozen crabmeat, or a mixture of brown and white meat if necessary. This dish looks very pretty served as a starter with the chilli sauce.

Makes 8 crabcakes

115g/4oz rice vermicelli noodles	1 tbsp fish sauce
oil for brushing	1 tbsp chopped fresh coriander
8 large fresh basil leaves	salt and freshly ground black pepper
180g/6oz crabmeat, preferably fresh	2 tsp cayenne pepper
5 tbsp coconut milk	120ml/4fl oz mayonnaise
2 tbsp red curry paste	1 fresh red chilli, seeded and finely
2 eggs, lightly beaten	chopped

Preheat the oven to 200°C/400°F/Gas 6. Cook the rice vermicelli in plenty of boiling water for 3 minutes, then drain well.

Brush a muffin tin or small bun tray lightly with oil, and line each tin with a single basil leaf. Divide the rice vermicelli among the tins and arrange into neat nests.

Put the crabmeat, coconut milk, red curry paste, eggs, fish sauce and coriander into a bowl and mix well. Season generously with salt and pepper. Spoon a little of the crab mixture into each noodle nest. Bake for 15 minutes or until the crab mixture has risen and set.

Meanwhile, combine the cayenne pepper, mayonnaise and chilli in a small bowl. Serve as a dip with the crabcakes.

YUNNAN NOODLE SOUP

For authenticity, serve this in soup cups with tight-fitting lids (you can find these in Oriental shops).

1.2 litres/2 pints strong chicken stock	3 tbsp sunflower or groundnut oil
4 shiitake mushrooms, halved	1 tsp sesame oil
100g/3¹/₂oz rice vermicelli noodles	2 tsp chilli oil
90g/3oz minced chicken	5cm/2in piece root ginger, grated
2 spring onions, finely chopped	1 garlic clove, crushed
2 tsp soy sauce	100g/3¹/₂oz watercress, chopped

Bring the stock to the boil in a large saucepan, and add the mushrooms, noodles, chicken, spring onions and soy sauce. Return to the boil, then remove from the heat. Cover and leave to stand for 5 minutes.

Meanwhile, put all the oils in a small saucepan with the ginger and garlic, and heat through until sizzling.

Stir the watercress into the soup and ladle into warmed serving bowls. Pour a little of the hot oil into each bowl, ensuring that the ginger and garlic are evenly distributed. Leave to stand for a further 3 minutes, then serve.

Right: Noodle Crabcakes

SALAD NOODLES

Noodles are perfect as a salad base, providing a contrasting background for the crunchiness and vibrant flavours of fresh vegetables, fruit and herbs, with piquant dressings. Noodles also give substance to salads, making excellent lunch or light supper dishes. All recipes serve 4–6 unless indicated otherwise.

RICE NOODLES WITH PEANUT SAUCE

Here is a deliciously rich and spicy version of satay sauce, used to dress rice noodles. This is a good accompaniment to a marinated chicken dish.

1/2 tsp cumin seeds
1/2 tsp coriander seeds
2 garlic cloves, crushed
1 small onion, quartered
1/2 red pepper, roughly chopped
1 tbsp lemon juice
1 tsp salt

1/2 fresh red chilli, seeded and sliced
120ml/4fl oz coconut milk
225g/8oz crunchy peanut butter
250ml/8fl oz water
115g/4oz rice thread noodles
1 tbsp chopped fresh coriander, to garnish

First, make the peanut sauce. Grind the cumin and coriander seeds in a spice mill or with a mortar and pestle. Mix with the garlic.

Switch on the food processor or blender and add the quartered onion through the feed tube, followed by the cumin mixture, the red pepper, lemon juice, salt, chilli, coconut milk and peanut butter.

When all the ingredients are fully combined, transfer to a saucepan and blend in the water. Bring to the boil and simmer for 2–3 minutes or until the sauce has a thin coating consistency. Set aside to cool. If the sauce thickens on cooling, thin it to the desired consistency with a little water.

Cook the noodles in plenty of boiling water according to packet instructions. Drain and refresh under cold running water. Drain well. Combine the noodles with the peanut sauce, transfer to a serving dish and garnish with chopped coriander.

PUMPKIN SALAD WITH NOODLES

Pumpkin is a versatile ingredient in salads, soups and stews. Here its slightly sweet flavour blends well with coriander and sesame.

500g/1lb 2oz pumpkin or butternut squash
225g/8oz soba noodles
2 tbsp sesame oil
4 tbsp sunflower oil
2 tsp red wine vinegar

1 tsp cayenne pepper, plus more to garnish
sea salt and freshly ground black pepper
4 tbsp chopped fresh coriander
2 tbsp sesame seeds, toasted

Preheat the oven to 180°C/350°F/Gas 4. Cut the pumpkin into 2 large pieces, or the butternut squash in half lengthways, and discard the seeds and fibres. Wrap in foil and bake for 45 minutes or until a fork pierces the flesh easily. Leave to cool, then peel away the skin and cut the flesh into 2.5cm/1in cubes.

Cook the noodles in plenty of boiling water for 4 minutes or according to packet instructions. Drain and refresh under cold running water. Drain well.

Combine the sesame oil, sunflower oil, red wine vinegar and cayenne pepper, and season to taste with salt and pepper. Toss the noodles with this dressing until they are evenly coated. Transfer to a serving dish and mix in the pumpkin cubes and coriander. Sprinkle with the sesame seeds and a pinch of cayenne pepper.

MINT AND LIME NOODLE SALAD

A fresh-tasting salad with a lot of crunch, from apples, celery and the white radish called mooli or daikon.

115g/4oz beancurd noodles
2 tbsp lime juice
salt and freshly ground black pepper
2 Granny Smith apples, cored and chopped

2 celery sticks, sliced
115g/4oz mooli, chopped
2 tbsp chopped fresh mint
115g/4oz alfalfa sprouts, to garnish

Pour boiling water over the noodles and leave to stand for 3 minutes or according to packet instructions. Drain well and set aside to cool.

Add the lime juice to the noodles and season well. Add the apples, celery, mooli and mint and toss together. Transfer to a serving bowl and sprinkle over the alfalfa sprouts. Serve immediately.

Right: Pumpkin Salad with Noodles

Above: Crunchy Green Salad

CRUNCHY GREEN SALAD

Often something fresh and crunchy is needed in an Oriental meal, and this subtly flavoured salad is just right. It would make a very pleasant refresher between courses, while you stir-fry the main course

Serves 6–8

115g/4oz egg thread noodles	*115g/4oz courgette, thinly sliced on a slant*
2 tbsp balsamic vinegar	*350g/12oz Chinese leaves, finely shredded*
2 tbsp olive oil	*115g/4oz small broccoli florets*
salt and freshly ground black pepper	*90g/3oz toasted cashews, roughly chopped*
115g/4oz asparagus	

Pour boiling water over the noodles and leave to stand for 3 minutes or according to packet instructions. Drain and refresh under cold running water. Drain well.

Combine the balsamic vinegar and olive oil, season to taste and toss with the noodles until they are evenly coated.

Blanch the asparagus in boiling water, refresh under cold running water and drain well. If the spears are large, cut into pieces. Toss together the noodles, asparagus, courgette, Chinese leaves and broccoli. Garnish with the toasted cashews and serve cold.

SPICY SALAD WITH GINGER AND CHILLI

Soba noodles have a definite, rich flavour, and they keep their lovely firm texture in a salad.

200g/7oz soba noodles	*1 fresh red chilli, finely chopped*
90g/3oz white cabbage, chopped	*2 tbsp chopped fresh coriander*
1 tsp turmeric	*2 spring onions, finely chopped*
1 garlic clove, crushed	*salt*
1 tsp grated root ginger	*juice of 1 lime*
1 tbsp shredded pickled ginger	*1/2 tsp onion pepper*
2 tbsp sunflower oil	

Cook the noodles in plenty of boiling water for 5 minutes or according to packet instructions. Drain, refresh under cold running water and drain well. Gently mix the chopped cabbage with the noodles.

Combine the turmeric, garlic, root and pickled ginger, oil, chilli, coriander and spring onions and season to taste with salt. Toss this mixture with the noodles until they are evenly coated. Add lime juice and onion pepper to taste and serve cold.

HERBED NOODLE SALAD

The zing that abundant fresh herbs give to a dish is quite different from the flavour given by a light sprinkling towards the end of cooking.

400g/14oz flat rice noodles	*4 tbsp chopped fresh basil*
2 tbsp sunflower oil	*salt and freshly ground black pepper*
1 red pepper, finely chopped	*1 fresh green chilli, halved and seeded*
4 tbsp chopped fresh coriander	*1 garlic clove, halved*
4 tbsp chopped fresh mint	*juice of 1 lemon*

Break the noodles into pieces about 5cm/2in long (it is easiest to do this while they are still in the packet). Cook them in boiling water for 3 minutes or according to packet instructions. Drain, refresh under cold running water and drain well.

Gently mix the noodles with the oil, red pepper and herbs. Season generously with salt and pepper.

Rub the inside of a serving bowl with the cut sides of the halved chilli and garlic clove; discard the chilli and garlic. Transfer the noodle salad to the serving bowl and sprinkle with the lemon juice

WHITE NOODLE CUCUMBER SALAD

A light but tasty salad, this combines the rich flavours of sesame with the coolness of cucumber.

500g/1lb 2oz cucumber
salt and freshly ground black pepper
75g/2¹/₂oz rice vermicelli noodles
2 tbsp sesame oil
2 tbsp rice vinegar

1 tbsp light soy sauce
juice of 1 lime
115g/4oz beansprouts
2 tbsp sesame seeds, toasted

Peel the cucumber and slice thinly. Rinse under cold running water, then mix with 4 teaspoons of salt. Leave to stand for 15 minutes, then rinse and drain well.

Pour boiling water over the noodles and leave to stand for 5 minutes or according to packet instructions. Drain and refresh under cold running water. Drain well.

Mix together the sesame oil, rice vinegar, soy sauce and lime juice. Season to taste, then toss with the noodles.

Stir the cucumber and beansprouts into the noodles. Serve sprinkled with the sesame seeds.

BEETROOT AND RADICCHIO SALAD

Beetroot was brought to the East by Russian invaders, and the Chinese, with their love of pickled vegetables, were soon preparing beetroot by this method.

150g/5oz mie noodles
1 tbsp light soy sauce
1 tbsp finely shredded pickled ginger
salt and freshly ground black pepper
2 tbsp sunflower oil

1 radicchio, shredded
90g/3oz pickled beetroot, rinsed
and quartered
3 spring onions, chopped
3 tbsp chopped fresh red basil

Pour boiling water over the noodles and leave to stand for 2 minutes or according to packet instructions. Rinse and drain well, trying to keep the noodles in the nest shapes. Toss the noodles gently with the soy sauce and pickled ginger, and season well.

Heat the oil in a frying pan, add the radicchio and cook over a moderate heat for 2–3 minutes, to soften. Remove from the heat and stir in the beetroot. Leave to cool.

Arrange the noodle nests in a serving dish. Spoon the beetroot, radicchio and spring onions over the dressed noodle nests and sprinkle with the red basil.

ONION NOODLE SALAD

The sweet yet piquant flavour of cooked white onions and spring onions perfectly complements egg thread noodles and mushrooms.

12 small white onions, peeled
4 tbsp olive oil
2 tbsp soy sauce
salt and freshly ground black pepper
12 spring onions, finely chopped

1 tbsp red wine vinegar
115g/4oz egg thread noodles
1 tbsp chopped fresh coriander
115g/4oz button mushrooms,
finely chopped

Preheat the oven to 180°C/350°F/Gas 4. Put the whole white onions in a roasting tin and toss with 1 tablespoon each of olive oil and soy sauce. Season well. Cover and bake for 20 minutes, basting often. Stir in half of the spring onions, baste well and return to the oven to bake for a further 10 minutes.

Meanwhile, combine the remaining oil and soy sauce with the vinegar and season this dressing well.

Pour boiling water over the noodles and leave to stand for 4 minutes or according to packet instructions. Drain and refresh under cold running water. Drain well. Toss with the dressing.

Leave the onions to cool for 5 minutes, then stir them into the noodles. Stir in the remaining spring onions, the coriander and mushrooms, and serve immediately.

Above: Beetroot and Radicchio Salad

21

LEMON PEPPER SALAD

When used as a major flavouring, pepper can add a surprising rich smokiness, and a tingle on the tongue. Measure the ingredients for the dressing quite carefully – success depends on the balance of flavours.

180g/6oz flat rice noodles	2 tbsp sunflower oil
grated zest of 1 lemon	1 tsp clear honey
3 tbsp lemon juice	salt
1 tsp mixed peppercorns, crushed	90g/3oz red radishes, sliced
2 tsp Japanese seven-pepper spice or	
lemon pepper	

Cook the noodles in plenty of boiling water for 5 minutes or according to packet instructions. Refresh under cold running water and drain.

Combine the lemon zest and juice, peppercorns, pepper, oil and honey. Season with salt to taste.

Toss the noodles with the lemon dressing until they are evenly coated. Fold in the sliced radishes, and serve cold.

CRISPY NOODLE SALAD

A fresh colourful salad with crunch, this is ideal for a summer buffet, or as an accompaniment to an Oriental curry or stir-fried dish.

60g/2oz rice vermicelli noodles	1 orange pepper, finely chopped
180g/6oz butter	115g/4oz button mushrooms, halved
2 tbsp sesame seeds, toasted	2 spring onions, finely chopped
2 tbsp sunflower seeds, toasted	sea salt and freshly ground black pepper
2 tbsp pumpkin seeds, toasted	shredded pickled ginger, to garnish
115g/4oz red cabbage, finely sliced	

Crush the rice vermicelli into small pieces (it is easiest to do while it is still in the packet, or in a plastic bag).

Melt the butter in a small saucepan and leave to cool slightly. As it cools you will notice that the solids drop to the bottom of the saucepan. Pour off the clear butter at the top – this is clarified butter – and discard the solids. Heat the clarified butter in a frying pan and fry the crushed noodles in batches, stirring constantly and gently. Drain the fried noodles on kitchen paper. Mix with the toasted seeds.

Combine the cabbage, orange pepper, mushrooms and spring onions in a salad bowl, and season with a little salt and pepper.

Just before serving, add the crisp noodles and toasted seeds to the vegetables and stir gently to mix. Serve immediately, before the noodles lose their crispness, garnished with a little pile of pickled ginger in the middle of the colourful salad.

JAPANESE UDON SALAD

Robust udon noodles are very satisfying in a salad. Fresh udon give a better result than dried ones because they are firmer and do not absorb so much dressing.

90g/3oz cucumber, finely sliced	60g/2oz pickled ginger, shredded
2 tbsp salt	115g/4oz Chinese leaves, shredded
225g/8oz udon noodles	2 tsp Japanese seven-pepper spice or
2 tsp sunflower oil	lemon pepper

Put the cucumber into a colander, sprinkle with the salt and leave to drain for 30 minutes. Rinse well under cold running water and pat dry with kitchen paper.

Cook the noodles in plenty of boiling water for 2 minutes or according to packet instructions. Drain well and toss with the oil.

Stir the cucumber and pickled ginger into the noodles, then add the Chinese leaves. Transfer to a serving bowl and sprinkle with the spice or lemon pepper.

RICE NOODLE SALAD

Here is a great salad for lunch or supper: crunchy vegetables and rice noodles in a dressing flavoured with lemon and ginger. You can substitute or add other vegetables, according to what is available.

Serves 6–8

2 tbsp lemon juice	200g/7oz flat rice noodles
1 tsp prepared mustard	115g/4oz beansprouts
1 tbsp grated root ginger	1 carrot, cut into matchsticks
3 tbsp sunflower oil	60g/2oz button mushrooms, halved
salt and freshly ground black pepper	200g/7oz canned water chestnuts, sliced

Put the lemon juice, mustard, ginger and oil into a bowl and whisk together. Season to taste with salt and pepper. Set aside.

Cook the noodles in plenty of boiling water according to packet instructions. Drain well and snip them into small pieces, then toss with the dressing.

Put all the vegetables into a serving bowl and add the noodles. Toss to mix the vegetables evenly with the noodles, and serve.

Right: Lemon Pepper Salad

SEAFOOD SALAD

Make this main-dish salad in the summer when palates need to be tempted with something cool and spicy. A generous bowl of garlic mayonnaise would be the perfect partner.

8 squid, cleaned, discarding the tentacles
2 tbsp mirin
2 tbsp rice vinegar
4 tbsp sunflower oil
1–2 fresh red chillies, seeded and chopped
180g/6oz medium egg noodles, broken into pieces
8 raw tiger prawns, peeled
1 red pepper, chopped

115g/4oz beansprouts
4 spring onions, sliced
180g/6oz crabmeat, preferably fresh
1 tbsp turmeric
2 garlic cloves, crushed
2 tsp ground coriander
1 tbsp lemon juice
salt

Cut the tapered end off each squid tube, and cut open down one side. Open out flat to form a square. Using a sharp knife, score a criss-cross pattern on the inside of the squid. Put into a bowl with the mirin, vinegar, half of the oil and the chillies. Leave to marinate for 1 hour.

Cook the egg noodles in boiling water for 5 minutes or according to packet instructions. Drain and refresh under cold water. Drain well.

Pour the squid and its marinade into a saucepan and add the prawns. Bring to the boil and simmer until tender (take care not to overcook). Drain and leave to cool.

Combine the red pepper, beansprouts, spring onions and noodles in a bowl. Add the squid, prawns and crabmeat.

Mix together the remaining oil with the turmeric, garlic and coriander and stir into the salad. Season to taste with lemon juice and salt. Transfer to a serving bowl and serve chilled.

MALAYSIAN COCONUT SALAD

Coconut milk is used extensively in Malaysian cooking, to give richness and enhance spicing. Here, coconut flakes are added for extra texture.

225g/8oz beancurd noodles
1 tbsp lime juice
1 tsp sesame oil
120ml/4fl oz coconut milk
pinch of sugar
pinch of salt
1 fresh red chilli, seeded and chopped
1 stalk lemon grass, lightly bruised
1 tsp turmeric

30g/1oz natural peanuts, roasted and chopped
6 baby sweetcorn, halved lengthways
115g/4oz beansprouts

TO GARNISH
60g/2oz coconut flakes
lime slices

Pour boiling water over the noodles and leave to stand for 3 minutes or according to packet instructions. Drain, rinse in cold water, drain well.

Combine the lime juice, sesame oil, coconut milk, sugar, salt and red chilli. Toss the noodles in this dressing.

Rub the lemon grass and turmeric around the inside of a serving bowl; discard the lemon grass. Toss the peanuts, baby sweetcorn and beansprouts with the noodles. Transfer to the serving bowl and garnish with the coconut flakes and lime slices.

AROMATIC NOODLE SALAD

This is a delicately flavoured salad, ideal as an accompaniment to richer dishes.

225g/8oz soba noodles
1 tbsp sunflower oil
4 tsp Sichuan peppercorns
1 tsp black peppercorns
2 tsp star anise seeds, crushed
115g/4oz beansprouts
425g/15oz canned lychees, drained and halved

1 star fruit, thinly sliced
1 tsp soy sauce
2 tbsp chopped fresh chervil
1 tbsp lemon juice
satsuma slices, to garnish

Cook the noodles in boiling water for 4 minutes or according to packet instructions. Drain, rinse under cold running water and drain well. Toss with the oil until it coats the noodles evenly.

Crush the Sichuan peppercorns and black peppercorns together. Combine these with the crushed star anise. Stir this spice mix through the noodles until evenly distributed.

Gently mix in the beansprouts, lychees and star fruit. Sprinkle over the soy sauce, chervil and lemon juice and toss gently. Serve cold, garnished with satsuma slices.

Right: *Malaysian Coconut Salad*

POULTRY

Versatile and popular, chicken is quick to cook and, in combination with noodles and intriguing Oriental flavours,

makes a satisfying midweek meal. With rich sauces, and poultry such as duck and quail, noodles are the ideal accompaniment.

All recipes serve 4–6.

CHICKEN CUPS

These are delicious served with a sweet chilli sauce. The cups can be prepared in advance and cooked just before serving.

225g/8oz medium egg noodles	1 egg, lightly beaten
350g/12oz minced chicken	30g/1oz sesame seeds, toasted
1/2 stalk lemon grass, finely chopped	1 tsp soy sauce
1 fresh green chilli, seeded and finely chopped	2 tbsp chopped fresh coriander
	2.5cm/1in piece root ginger, grated
250ml/8fl oz coconut milk	8 large fresh basil leaves

Preheat the oven to 180°C/350°F/Gas 4. Cook the noodles in plenty of boiling water for 5 minutes or according to packet instructions. Rinse and drain well.

Combine the chicken with the lemon grass, chilli, coconut milk, egg, sesame seeds, soy sauce, chopped coriander and ginger in a large bowl.

Line the bottom of 8 muffin tins or deep bun tins with a basil leaf. Spoon the noodles around the sides. Spoon the chicken mixture into the centre. Bake for 15 minutes or until the chicken mixture is cooked.

SESAME CHICKEN NOODLES

Sesame and chicken are a simple but effective flavour combination.

225g/8oz beancurd noodles	350g/12oz boneless chicken, cut into strips
3 tbsp sunflower oil	30g/1oz sesame seeds, toasted
2 tsp sesame oil	
1 garlic clove, crushed	TO SERVE
350g/12oz Chinese leaves, shredded	prawn crackers
3 spring onions, sliced	chilli sauce

Pour boiling water over the noodles and leave to stand for 3–5 minutes or according to packet instructions. Drain.

Heat the sunflower oil, sesame oil and garlic in a wok or large open pan. When it is hot, add the Chinese leaves and stir-fry for 2 minutes.

Stir in the spring onions, chicken, sesame seeds and the noodles. Stir-fry over a high heat for about 3 minutes, using two spoons to lift and stir the mixture, to allow any excess liquid to evaporate so that the noodles do not become soggy. When the chicken is cooked and the noodles are hot, serve immediately, accompanied by prawn crackers and chilli sauce.

CHICKEN IN THE BASKET

Deep-fried noodles are used as a basket to hold stir-fried chicken. To make the noodle baskets, you will need a cup-shaped wire draining spoon; this can be bought in any Oriental supermarket.

115g/4oz rice vermicelli noodles	1 tsp light soft brown sugar
450g/1lb boneless chicken thighs, sliced	1 tbsp fish sauce
1 garlic clove, crushed	2 tbsp red curry paste
2.5cm/1in piece root ginger, grated	200ml/7fl oz coconut milk
oil for deep-frying	about 2 tbsp oyster sauce
1 tsp sesame oil	red pepper, finely sliced, to garnish
3 spring onions, finely sliced	

Cover the noodles with boiling water and leave to stand for 1 minute, then drain well (remove as much moisture as possible because any left will make the hot frying oil spit).

Toss the chicken with the garlic and ginger and set aside while you prepare the baskets.

Heat oil in a wok or deep fat fryer. Test the temperature with a piece of rice noodle: if it immediately rises to the surface and expands, the oil is ready.; if not, wait a few moments and test again. Once the oil is hot, arrange one-sixth of the noodles in the wire draining spoon, pushing them against the sides and making a hollow in the middle. Immerse the spoon in the hot oil and fry for 10 seconds or until the shape of the noodle basket is set. Slip the basket off the spoon and turn it over in the oil. Cook for a little longer or until the basket is golden brown all over. Drain on plenty of kitchen paper, and keep warm. Shape and fry the remaining noodle baskets.

Pour off all but 1 tablespoon of the oil from the wok. Add the sesame oil and when it is hot, add the chicken and spring onions and stir-fry over a high heat for 2 minutes. Then add the sugar, fish sauce, curry paste and coconut milk. Stir for 1 minute or until the sauce begins to thicken. Add oyster sauce to taste.

Divide the chicken mixture among the deep-fried noodle baskets and serve, garnished with strips of red pepper.

CHICKEN NOODLE NESTS

Fried noodles, packed in long-life containers, are available in Oriental shops, but they cannot compare to freshly made, and would not be suitable for this recipe.

Makes 4 nests

115g/4oz flat rice noodles	1 tsp salt
90g/3oz instant mashed potato mix, reconstituted	450g/1 lb chicken, cut into strips about 1 x 4cm/³/8 x 1¹/2in
1 tsp coriander seeds	1 garlic clove, crushed
1 tsp cumin seeds	2.5cm/1in piece root ginger, grated
4 cloves	2 dried red chillies, seeded and sliced
1 whole star anise	4 spring onions, sliced
1 tsp white peppercorns	30g/1oz fresh coriander, coarsely
oil for deep-frying	chopped

Dip the rice noodles quickly into cold water, then drain and break into 5cm/2in pieces.

On a work surface or tray, space out 8 heaped teaspoons of the instant potato, and press some noodles into each heap. Put another teaspoon of instant potato on top of each heap and press in some more noodles. Mould roughly into 7.5cm/3in round nests; you may need to shape the nests in your hands.

Grind together the coriander seeds, cumin seeds, cloves, star anise and peppercorns in a mortar and pestle or spice grinder. Set aside.

Heat 2.5cm/1in of oil in a wok or deep frying pan. Test the temperature with a piece of noodle: if it does not immediately rise to the surface, the oil is not hot enough, so wait a minute and try again. When the oil is hot enough, drop in one nest and gently flatten it between two spoons to hold the shape. Fry, turning it over once, until it is golden brown. Remove and drain on plenty of kitchen paper. Fry the remaining nests, then season with salt and keep them warm.

Pour off all but 2 tablespoons of the oil from the wok. Add the chicken, garlic, ginger and chillies and stir-fry until cooked. Stir in the ground spices. Add the spring onions and stir-fry for a further 2 minutes. Add the coriander.

Put a deep-fried noodle nest on each plate and spoon some chicken on top. Top with another deep-fried nest and serve.

CHINESE QUAILS ON A BED OF NOODLES

Try to use part-boned quails if you can find them – they are much easier to eat.

4 tbsp clear honey	2 tbsp sunflower oil
seeds from 4 star anise, crushed	4 spring onions, each cut into 3 pieces
1 tsp tamarind paste	2 celery sticks, cut into matchsticks
2 tbsp soy sauce	2 carrots, cut into matchsticks, or
2 tbsp dry sherry	8 baby carrots
2 tbsp yellow bean sauce	350g/12oz Chinese flat wheat noodles
1 bay leaf	2 courgettes, cut into thin slices lengthways
4 garlic cloves, unpeeled, crushed lightly	using a vegetable peeler
with the back of a knife	3 tbsp chopped fresh coriander leaves
4 quails	2 star fruit, sliced, to garnish

Combine the honey, crushed star anise seeds, tamarind, soy sauce, sherry, yellow bean sauce and bay leaf, and set aside.

Put a garlic clove into the cavity of each quail. Heat the oil in a wok or large open pan. When it is hot, add the quails and fry over a high heat until browned on all sides.

Add the honey paste and stir to coat the quails all over. Cover the wok and cook over a high heat for 5 minutes. Remove the cover and cook for a further 5 minutes, turning the quails frequently and basting to glaze them. Add the spring onions, celery and carrots and cook, uncovered, for a further 5 minutes, stirring frequently.

Meanwhile, cook the noodles in plenty of boiling water for 4 minutes or according to packet instructions. When the noodles are cooked, add the courgette slices to the boiling water, then immediately drain the noodles and courgettes.

Serve the quails on a bed of the courgette noodles, with the vegetables arranged around them. Garnish with the coriander and star fruit.

Right: *Chinese Quails on a Bed of Noodles*

STEAMED LETTUCE PARCELS

Do not worry if the parcels are not particularly neat before they go into the steamer; they fuse together as they steam.

60g/2oz beancurd noodles	*60g/2oz firm tofu, finely diced*
180g/6oz minced chicken	*2 round lettuces*
1/2 tsp white peppercorns, crushed	
4 tsp light soy sauce	*TO SERVE*
4 tsp grated root ginger	*a selection of pickled vegetables*
100g/3 1/2oz canned water chestnuts,	*soy sauce*
finely chopped	

Pour boiling water over the noodles and leave to stand for 3–5 minutes or according to packet instructions. Drain and rinse, then drain well. Chop the noodles into 2.5cm/1in pieces and set aside.

Put the chicken into a bowl with the peppercorns, soy sauce, ginger, water chestnuts and tofu. Mix well, then stir in the noodles.

Separate the lettuce leaves and rinse well. Remove the central stalks. Gently pull out the edges of the leaves, so they lie flat. Spoon 1 tablespoon of the chicken mixture into the middle of each leaf and wrap up neatly. If the leaves are small, you may need to use two for a parcel. Refrigerate until ready to cook.

Steam the parcels for 15–20 minutes or until the chicken is cooked through; they may need longer if the parcels have been refrigerated for a while. Serve hot, accompanied by pickled vegetables and soy sauce.

ICED LEMON CHICKEN

This is a delicious dish for parties, especially on a hot summer day.

3 lemons	*2 tbsp sunflower oil*
3 thick slices root ginger	*2 tsp white wine vinegar*
4 boneless chicken breasts	*2 tsp grated root ginger*
1 bay leaf	*2 tsp light soy sauce*
1 tbsp Japanese seven-spice pepper or	*1 tsp caster sugar*
lemon pepper	*2 spring onions, finely chopped*
180g/6oz flat rice noodles	*salt and freshly ground black pepper*
115g/4oz beansprouts	*ice, to serve*

Prick one of the lemons all over with a skewer, and put it into a large pan with the ginger slices, chicken breasts, bay leaf and enough water to cover. Bring to the boil, then poach gently for about 15 minutes or until the chicken is just cooked.

Drain the chicken and leave to cool, then sprinkle with the spice pepper. Grate the zest of the remaining lemons over the chicken.

Cook the noodles in boiling water according to packet instructions. Drain, rinse well and drain again. Toss with the beansprouts.

Squeeze 1 tablespoon juice from a lemon, and put into a bowl with the oil and vinegar. Add the grated ginger, soy sauce, sugar and spring onions. Whisk well to make a thick dressing. Taste and season.

Put a layer of ice in a serving bowl. Spoon in the noodles and beansprouts. Slice each chicken breast into 6 pieces, and arrange on the noodles. Spoon on the dressing and serve at once, before the ice melts.

SATAY CHICKEN WITH NOODLES

The chicken is marinated and cooked on wooden skewers – available from Oriental stores – which must be soaked in water for 20 minutes before use.

700g/1 1/2lb boneless chicken, cut	*2 tbsp soy sauce*
into 7.5cm/3in strips	*2 tbsp sunflower oil*
1 small onion, sliced	*1 tbsp lemon juice*
2 garlic cloves, crushed	*1 tsp dark soft brown sugar*
1 tsp ground coriander	*225g/8oz egg thread noodles*
1 tsp ground cumin	*2 tbsp chopped fresh coriander*
2 fresh red chillies, seeded and roughly	*2 tbsp chopped fresh mint*
chopped	*2 spring onions, finely sliced*
2.5cm/1in piece root ginger, grated	

FOR THE PEANUT SAUCE

1 small onion, quartered	*1 tbsp lemon juice*
2 garlic cloves, crushed	*1 tsp salt*
1 tsp coriander seeds	*120ml/4fl oz coconut milk*
1 tsp cumin seeds	*225g/8oz crunchy peanut butter*
1/2 fresh red chilli	*250ml/8fl oz water*

Thread the chicken on to the soaked skewers.

Combine the onion, garlic, ground coriander and cumin, chillies, ginger, soy sauce, oil, lemon juice and brown sugar in a shallow dish. Add the chicken skewers and refrigerate for 2 hours.

Meanwhile, make the peanut sauce. In a food processor, combine the onion quarters, garlic, spices and chilli. Add the remaining sauce ingredients, except the water, in the order given, and process until well mixed. Transfer to a saucepan and blend in the water. Bring to a gentle boil and simmer until thick. Pour into a serving bowl and set aside.

Preheat the grill to medium-hot. Grill the chicken skewers for 10 minutes, turning and basting frequently.

Meanwhile, pour boiling water over the noodles and leave to stand for 3 minutes or according to packet instructions. Drain and stir in the chopped coriander and mint and sliced spring onions.

Serve the chicken satay sticks on a bed of noodles, accompanied by the peanut sauce.

Right: Steamed Lettuce Parcels

CHILLI CHICKEN WITH NOODLES

This recipe is full of flavour and easily made – it's great for a midweek supper, served with a green salad.

225g/8oz medium egg noodles	1/2 tsp freshly ground black pepper
1 tbsp sunflower oil	350g/12oz boneless chicken, either thigh
1 red pepper, finely diced	or breast, cut into 5cm/2in strips
6 spring onions, finely sliced	salt
1 tsp ground coriander	juice of 2 limes
2 tsp chilli flakes or chilli sauce	115g/4oz beansprouts

Cook the noodles in plenty of boiling water for 5 minutes or according to packet instructions. Drain.

Heat the oil in a wok or large open pan, add the red pepper and spring onions and stir-fry over a high heat for 1 minute. Add the ground coriander, chilli flakes or sauce and black pepper.

Add the chicken and stir-fry until just cooked and coated with the spice mixture. Add salt to taste and stir in the lime juice, beansprouts and noodles. Serve immediately.

CHICKEN RAMEN

If you are a noodle fanatic, you'll soon be hooked on ramen dishes because they can be altered so easily, according to the ingredients you have on hand and the flavourings you particularly like.

150ml/5fl oz mirin	4 boneless chicken breasts, fillets removed
150ml/5fl oz soy sauce	60g/2oz konbu
150ml/5fl oz chicken stock	1 litre/13/4 pints dashi broth
1 tbsp caster sugar	400g/14oz ramen noodles

TO SERVE

2 spring onions, finely sliced	grated root ginger
soy sauce	chilli oil

Put the mirin into a small saucepan, bring to the boil and boil to reduce by half. Remove from the heat and add the soy sauce, chicken stock and sugar. Pour into a shallow dish and leave the chicken to marinate in this mixture for 1 hour only.

Soak the konbu in warm water for 15 minutes; drain and slice finely.

Bring the dashi broth to the boil, add the noodles and cook for 2 minutes. Drain, reserving the broth. Keep both noodles and broth hot.

Heat a wok or large open pan to searing temperature. Put in the marinated chicken breasts and press down with a spatula. Cook for 5 minutes, turning once. This fast cooking over a high heat keeps the chicken moist on the inside and retains maximum flavour.

Arrange the noodles in serving bowls and add a few pieces of soaked konbu. Pour the hot broth over the noodles. Slice the chicken breasts and arrange on top of the noodles. Serve immediately, accompanied by spring onions, soy sauce, ginger and chilli oil, to be added according to personal taste.

RED CURRY WITH NOODLES

Red curry paste can be bought ready-made, but when you have tasted the freshly made version, there is no going back! The paste will keep for up to 3 weeks in a sealed jar in the refrigerator. Alternatively it can be frozen; be sure to wrap the portions very well, otherwise the pungent flavour will permeate other foods in the freezer.

700g/11/2lb boneless chicken thighs	115g/4oz mange tout
or breast, cut into strips	225g/8oz medium egg noodles
250ml/8fl oz coconut milk	1 tbsp chopped fresh coriander
1/4 tsp light soy sauce	10 fresh basil leaves, roughly chopped
60g/2oz baby sweetcorn, halved	
lengthways	

FOR THE RED CURRY PASTE

6 fresh or dried red chillies, halved,	grated zest of 1 lime
seeded and blanched	4 garlic cloves, chopped
2 tsp cumin seeds	3 shallots, chopped
2 tsp coriander seeds	2 kaffir lime leaves, mid rib removed,
2.5cm/1in piece galangal, chopped	shredded
1/2 stalk lemon grass, chopped	1 tbsp sunflower oil
1 tsp salt	

To make the curry paste, grind all the ingredients together in a large pestle and mortar, food processor or spice grinder.

Heat a wok or large heavy frying pan over a high heat and stir-fry 3 tablespoons of the red curry paste until fragrant. Add the chicken strips and stir-fry over a high heat until sealed on all sides.

Add the coconut milk, soy sauce, baby sweetcorn and mange tout. Bring to a gentle boil and simmer for 10 minutes or until the vegetables are cooked but still crisp.

Meanwhile, cook the noodles in plenty of boiling water for 5 minutes or according to packet instructions. Drain and keep warm.

Stir the coriander and basil into the curry. Divide the noodles among the serving bowls and spoon the hot curry on top.

Right: Chicken Ramen

FISH & SHELLFISH

Seafood is a great favourite in Southeast Asia and the Far East; fish and shellfish – particularly prawns and squid – are frequently used in noodle dishes. Cooking times are usually very short, so the seafood retains its succulent texture and fresh flavour.

All recipes serve 4–6.

INDONESIAN STIR-FRIED NOODLES

This dish, called Mee Goreng, is eaten all over Indonesia, Singapore and Malaysia, as is its rice equivalent, Nasi Goreng.

225g/8oz egg thread noodles
1 egg
3 tbsp water
2 tbsp sunflower oil
4 shallots, sliced
2 garlic cloves, crushed
1 green pepper, finely chopped
1 red pepper, finely chopped
1 tsp ground coriander
1 tsp ground cumin
1 tsp grated root ginger
3 fresh red chillies, sliced
1 tsp shrimp paste
115g/4oz boneless chicken breast, diced
115g/4oz boneless pork, diced

180g/6oz peeled raw tiger prawns, or cooked peeled prawns
1 tbsp Indonesian soy sauce (kecap manis)
salt
fresh coriander leaves, to garnish

FOR THE GARNISHES
75g/2¹/₂oz cucumber, thinly sliced
rice vinegar
sugar
3 tbsp chopped roasted peanuts
2 spring onions, finely sliced
3 tomatoes, thinly sliced
prawn crackers

Cook the noodles in plenty of boiling water for 3 minutes or according to packet instructions. Drain and rinse well, then drain again.

Lightly beat the egg with the water. Put a few drops of the oil into a wok and, when it is quite hot, make a very thin omelette with the egg mixture. Roll up and leave to cool. When cold, cut into thin strips.

To prepare the garnishes, lightly pickle the cucumber in equal quantities of rice vinegar and sugar for 5 minutes, then drain. Put into a serving dish. Put the remaining garnishes in individual serving dishes.

Heat the remaining oil in the wok, add the shallots and garlic and stir-fry over a high heat for 2–3 minutes or until soft. Add the green and red peppers and stir-fry for 1 minute, then add the ground coriander and cumin, ginger, chillies and shrimp paste. Stir well. Add the chicken and pork. If using raw prawns add them at this stage; if using cooked prawns, add at the end of cooking, with the noodles. Stir-fry until the chicken, pork and prawns are cooked.

Add the noodles and mix in, using two spoons to lift and stir until they are evenly coated with the sauce and hot through. Add the soy sauce and salt to taste. Scatter over some coriander leaves and the omelette strips, and serve hot, with the garnishes.

SALMON COCONUT CURRY

A rich, mild curry for a special occasion. It is equally good with prawns or any firm-fleshed fish, such as monkfish.

1 tbsp sunflower oil
1 onion, chopped
1 garlic clove, chopped
1 fresh green chilli, seeded and chopped
2.5cm/1in piece root ginger, chopped
1 tsp turmeric
1 tsp paprika
pinch of ground cumin

600g/1¹/₄lb salmon, diced
120ml/4fl oz coconut milk
200g/7oz canned chopped tomatoes
juice of 1 lemon
salt and freshly ground black pepper
225g/8oz rice thread noodles
2 tbsp chopped fresh coriander

Heat the oil in a wok or large open pan. Add the onion, garlic, chilli and ginger, then stir in the turmeric, paprika and cumin. Cook over a gentle heat for 2 minutes, stirring occasionally.

Increase the heat and add the salmon. Stir gently, until the salmon is coated in the spices and sealed on all sides. Add the coconut cream and tomatoes, and season to taste with lemon juice, salt and pepper. Reduce the heat and leave to simmer for 2–3 minutes.

Meanwhile, cook the noodles in plenty of boiling water for 3 minutes or according to packet instructions. Drain well

Spoon the curry over the noodles and serve immediately, garnished with the chopped coriander.

CANTONESE OYSTER NOODLES

A wide variety of fresh seafood is available in southern China, and is often eaten in simple dishes with egg noodles, such as the one here. If fresh oysters are not available, you can substitute canned.

150g/5oz egg thread noodles	24 fresh oysters, shelled
2 tbsp sunflower oil	3 tbsp dry sherry
4 spring onions, finely sliced	1 tbsp light soy sauce
2 garlic cloves, crushed	

Pour boiling water over the noodles to cover them and leave to stand for 3 minutes or according to packet instructions. Drain and rinse, then drain again well. Keep warm.

Heat the oil in a wok or large open pan and stir-fry the spring onions and garlic over moderate heat for 1 minute; do not let the garlic brown too much.

Add the oysters and sherry and stir-fry over a high heat for 1 minute. Stir in the soy sauce. Spoon the oysters over the noodles and serve.

SWORDFISH WITH CUCUMBER NOODLE CUPS

Swordfish has a deliciously meaty texture. If possible, choose larger steaks for the best flavour and texture. The cucumber sauce also works well with quickly cooked beef, pork, trout and shellfish.

2 tbsp mirin or dry sherry	2 tbsp chopped capers
1 tbsp black peppercorns, crushed	2 tbsp chopped fresh chives
1 tbsp sunflower oil	1 tsp wine vinegar
4 swordfish steaks, weighing about	3 tbsp mayonnaise
180g/6oz each	1 tbsp thickened double cream
1/2 cucumber, diced	115g/4oz rice thread noodles
1 tbsp salt	

Combine the mirin, crushed peppercorns and oil. Put the swordfish in a non-metallic dish and pour over the oil mixture. Turn the fish to coat evenly with the marinade. Cover and refrigerate for up to 8 hours.

Put the diced cucumber in a bowl with the salt, mix well and leave for 20 minutes, then drain and rinse in a sieve. Put the cucumber in a bowl and add the capers, chives and wine vinegar. Combine the mayonnaise and double cream and stir into the cucumber mixture. Set aside.

Preheat the oven to 220°C/425°F/Gas 7. Wrap each piece of swordfish individually in foil, and bake for 10 minutes.

Meanwhile, pour boiling water over the noodles to cover them and leave to stand for 3–5 minutes or according to packet instructions. Drain well and keep warm.

Divide the noodles among the serving plates, making a compact pile on each. With the handle of a wooden spoon, or your thumb, make a deep indentation in each pile of noodles. Spoon the cucumber sauce into this indentation. Serve alongside the swordfish.

PRAWN TEMPURA SOBA

Tempura batter is very different from a Western fritter or frying batter in that it is very light and not particularly well blended. It should be used as soon as it is made.

oil for deep-frying	1 tbsp finely shredded nori
12–18 raw tiger prawns, peeled	1 tbsp finely grated root ginger
1 litre/1³/4 pints dashi broth	3 spring onions, finely chopped
500g/1lb 2oz soba noodles	

FOR THE DIPPING SAUCE

3 tbsp mirin or dry sherry	3 tbsp dried bonito flakes
3 tbsp Japanese soy sauce	about 1 tsp wasabi paste
185ml/6fl oz chicken stock	pinch of salt

FOR THE BATTER

1 egg yolk	pinch of bicarbonate of soda
450ml/15fl oz ice-cold water	180g/6oz plain flour

First, make the dipping sauce. Put the mirin into a small saucepan, bring to the boil and boil to reduce by half. Add the soy sauce, chicken stock and bonito flakes, and bring back to a gentle boil. Immediately remove from the heat and strain. Add wasabi paste and salt to taste. Transfer to a serving bowl and set aside.

Heat oil in a wok or deep fat fryer to about 180°C/350°F. To make the batter, combine the egg yolk and water in a bowl and beat well with a fork. Sift in the bicarbonate of soda and flour. Beat well with a fork. Dip the prawns into the batter and then immediately deep-fry them in the hot oil until puffed and golden brown. Drain on kitchen paper and keep warm.

Heat the dashi broth. Meanwhile, cook the noodles in boiling water for 4 minutes or according to packet instructions; drain.

Spoon the noodles into warmed serving bowls and ladle in the hot broth. Sprinkle with the shredded nori, ginger and spring onions. Top each bowl with three prawns. Serve at once, with the dipping sauce.

CHILLI GARLIC PRAWNS

The rich combination of juicy prawns, garlic and chillies is a favourite with many people. Here it is served on a bed of rice noodles.

225g/8oz flat rice noodles	pinch of salt
60g/2oz butter	freshly ground black pepper
2 garlic cloves, crushed	300g/10oz peeled raw tiger prawns
2 fresh red chillies, finely chopped	4 tbsp chopped fresh coriander

Pour boiling water over the noodles to cover them; leave to stand for 5 minutes or according to packet instructions. Drain well; keep warm.

Heat the butter in a wok or large open pan. When it is foaming add the garlic and chillies. Season and add the prawns. Stir-fry over a high heat for 2 minutes or until cooked.

Serve the prawns on the noodles, sprinkled liberally with coriander.

Right: *Chilli Garlic Prawns*

Saffron Noodles with Red Snapper

This recipe comes from Australia, where they use seafood in the most wonderful and imaginative ways!

2 tbsp extra virgin olive oil
3 tomatoes, chopped
100g/3½oz pitted black olives, roughly chopped
1 tbsp chopped capers
salt and freshly ground black pepper
4–6 red snapper fillets, weighing about 180g/6 oz each

2 tsp packed saffron threads
1 tbsp boiling water
225g/8oz mie noodles
1 tbsp chopped fresh flat-leaf parsley
1 tbsp lemon juice

Preheat the oven to 180°C/350°F/Gas 4. Gently heat the olive oil in a saucepan, and stir in the tomatoes, olives and capers. Season generously with salt and black pepper. Remove from the heat.

Arrange the fish fillets on a baking tray. Spoon over the tomato mixture, pressing it well into the flesh. Bake the fish for 10 minutes or until just cooked.

Meanwhile, lightly crush the saffron threads, and leave to infuse in the boiling water.

Pour boiling water over the noodles and leave to stand according to the packet instructions. Drain well, keeping the nests together as much as possible. Toss the noodles gently with the saffron liquid to colour them evenly. Season generously with black pepper.

Divide the saffron noodles among the serving plates, and place a fish fillet on each bed of noodles. Stir the parsley and lemon juice into the sauce left in the baking tray, taste and adjust the seasoning and spoon over the fish fillets.

Seafood Ramen

This is a deliciously filling Japanese noodle stew, in which the flavours are subtle but intense. Nori, a sea vegetable sold dried in very thin sheets, adds an unusual bittersweet flavour.

1.5 litres/2½ pints fish stock
8–12 raw tiger prawns, peeled
4–6 scallops, shelled
12–18 baby squid , cleaned, discarding the tentacles, bodies sliced
400g/14oz ramen noodles
about 2 tbsp soy sauce

4–6 thin slices Japanese fishcake – either kamaboko or naruto
1 sheet nori, flaked

TO SERVE
2 spring onions, finely chopped
grated root ginger
soy sauce

Heat the fish stock to boiling, and steam the prawns, scallops and squid over the stock for 4 minutes.

Meanwhile, cook the noodles in plenty of boiling water for 2 minutes or according to packet instructions. Drain. Divide the noodles among the serving bowls.

Flavour the fish stock with soy sauce to taste and ladle over the noodles. Arrange the prawns, scallops, squid and Japanese fishcake on top. Scatter with the nori flakes. Serve immediately, accompanied by the spring onions, grated ginger and soy sauce, to be added according to personal taste.

Singapore Noodles

When eaten on the street in Singapore, these noodles come in many variations, depending on what the stallholder has available that day. Feel free to experiment with the ingredients here.

225g/8oz rice thread noodles
2 tbsp sunflower oil
2 shallots, sliced
2 garlic cloves, crushed
2 tbsp grated root ginger
½ red pepper, shredded
½ green pepper, shredded
1 tsp chilli flakes
1 tbsp ground coriander

115g/4oz boneless pork, diced
180g/6oz boneless chicken, diced
180g/6oz peeled raw prawns, diced, or cooked peeled prawns
60g/2oz thawed frozen peas
1 tbsp liquid seasoning, such as Maggi
juice of 1 lemon
3 tbsp chopped fresh coriander

Pour boiling water over the noodles to cover them; leave to stand for 4 minutes or according to packet instructions. Drain well and set aside.

Heat the oil in a wok, add the shallots, garlic, ginger, red pepper, green pepper and chilli flakes and stir-fry over a high heat for 2 minutes or until the shallots are softened. Stir in the ground coriander, followed by the pork, chicken and raw prawns; if using cooked prawns, add them at the end of cooking, with the noodles. Stir-fry over a high heat for 4 minutes or until the pork is cooked.

Add the noodles and peas to the wok and use two spoons to lift and stir until the noodles are coated evenly with the sauce and hot through. Add the liquid seasoning and lemon juice. Serve hot, garnished with the chopped coriander.

SHELLFISH NOODLES

This dish looks very colourful, with the mussels, cockles and prawns still in their shells. However, you will need to provide finger bowls!.

1.35kg/3lb mixed shellfish, such as
live mussels and cockles,
raw tiger prawns in their shells,
scallops, preferably with their corals
2 tbsp sunflower oil
2 spring onions, finely chopped
1 tbsp finely chopped root ginger
1–2 fresh red chillies, finely chopped

1 garlic clove, crushed
1 tsp turmeric
4 tomatoes, skinned, seeded and chopped
225g/8oz rice vermicelli noodles
4 tbsp chopped fresh mixed herbs,
such as chives, parsley, chervil
salt and freshly ground black pepper

Prepare the shellfish according to type: scrub the mussels and cockle shells, scraping off any barnacles, and wash in several changes of fresh cold water; rinse the prawns and scallops and pat dry.

Heat the oil in a wok or large open pan, add the spring onions, ginger, chillies, garlic, turmeric and tomatoes and stir-fry over a high heat for 2 minutes. Reduce the heat, add the shellfish, cover the wok and cook for 5 minutes, stirring frequently.

Meanwhile, pour boiling water over the noodles to cover them; leave to stand for 4 minutes or according to packet instructions. Drain well and toss with the herbs.

Discard any unopened shellfish, taste the sauce and adjust the seasoning if necessary, then serve immediately, on a bed of noodles.

SAFFRON SCALLOPS ON A BED OF NOODLES

This is a very pretty dish, with creamy-coloured scallops, tomato and chives in a saffron-yellow sauce. Use fresh scallops if possible.

1 tsp saffron threads, lightly crushed
2 tbsp warm water
225g/8oz medium egg noodles
60g/2oz butter
16 large scallops, shelled, with the corals

1 spring onion, finely sliced
3 tomatoes, skinned, seeded and chopped
3 tbsp chopped fresh chives
pinch of salt

Combine the saffron and warm water, and leave to infuse.

Cook the noodles in plenty of boiling water for 5 minutes or according to packet instructions. Drain well and keep warm.

Melt the butter in a pan just large enough to hold all of the scallops. Stir in the saffron liquid. When the butter is medium-hot, add the scallops, spring onion, tomatoes and chives. Cover and cook over a moderate heat for 7 minutes. Season with a little salt.

Spoon the scallops and sauce over the noodles and serve.

ICED LOBSTER SALAD

A sophisticated Pacific Rim salad idea – the perfect way to prepare lobster in the summer. You can use two 450g/1lb lobsters if you prefer.

115g/4oz rice vermicelli noodles
900g/2lb lobster, cooked
sliced pickled ginger, finely chopped

Japanese seven-pepper spice or lemon pepper
2 tbsp chopped fresh chervil
2 tbsp chopped fresh red basil

Break the vermicelli into little pieces while it is still in the packet. Pour over boiling water to cover; leave to stand for 3 minutes or according to packet instructions. Drain and rinse, then drain well.

Remove the legs from the lobster, close to the body. Snap each leg in half at the joint and remove the meat with a skewer. Break each claw off near the body, and crack the claw shell with a mallet. Remove the meat from each claw in one piece if possible, including the meat from the pincers. Discard the blade that you will find in the claw meat.

Cut off the head, and lay the lobster on its back. Use a heavy knife or kitchen scissors to cut through the belly shell down the centre. Pull open the shell and remove the meat in one piece. Cut the meat across into 8 equal pieces.

Put a layer of ice in a serving dish and spoon the rice vermicelli over it. Sprinkle with some pickled ginger. Arrange the pieces of lobster, including the meat from the claws and legs, neatly over the top. Sprinkle with Japanese pepper, chervil and red basil, and serve immediately, before the ice melts.

Above: Saffron Noodles with Red Snapper

TERIYAKI SALMON WITH NOODLES

Ready-made teriyaki marinade and sauce can be bought in supermarkets, but a better result and a fuller flavour will be achieved by making your own.

75ml/3fl oz mirin or medium dry sherry	225g/8oz medium egg noodles
75 ml/3fl oz light soy sauce	2 tbsp sesame oil
75 ml/3fl oz chicken stock	2 tbsp finely chopped fresh chives
4 salmon fillets, weighing about	3 spring onions, finely chopped
180g/6oz each	

First, make the teriyaki sauce. Put the mirin or sherry in a saucepan, bring to the boil and simmer for 2 minutes or until reduced by half. Add the soy sauce and stock. Remove from the heat.

Preheat the grill to very hot, and line the grill pan with foil. Arrange the salmon fillets in the pan and brush with the teriyaki sauce. Grill for 5–6 minutes on each side, basting often with the sauce.

Meanwhile, cook the noodles in plenty of boiling water for 5 minutes or according to packet instructions. Drain and stir in the sesame oil, chives and spring onions.

Serve the salmon on a bed of piping hot noodles, accompanied by any remaining teriyaki sauce.

SPICY SHRIMP NOODLES

Fresh tiny brown shrimps – the kind used for making potted shrimps – are ideal for this recipe, although you could also use canned shrimps or peeled cooked prawns.

60g/2oz beancurd noodles	1 tsp turmeric
1 tbsp sunflower oil	pinch of salt
2 shallots, finely chopped	1 tsp chilli flakes
2 tsp ground coriander	1 garlic clove, crushed
1/2 tsp ground cumin	1 tbsp lemon juice
1/2 tsp black pepper	225g/8oz tiny brown shrimps

Cover the noodles with boiling water and leave to stand for 3 minutes or according to packet instructions. Drain well and keep warm.

Heat the oil in a wok or large open frying pan, add the shallots and cook over a moderate heat for 10 minutes, without browning. Add the coriander, cumin, pepper, turmeric, salt, chilli flakes and, lastly, the garlic. Squeeze over the lemon juice and stir in the shrimps.

As soon as the shrimp mixture is hot through, toss with the noodles and serve immediately.

MALAYSIAN SWEET CURRY

Called Laksa Lemak in Malaysia, this is traditionally made just with fish, but chicken is a good addition. The texture of this curry is quite watery – once the noodles have been slurped and the chicken eaten, the coconut soup/sauce is sipped from the bowl.

1 chicken, weighing about 1kg/2 1/4lb	115g/4oz flat rice noodles
2 tbsp sunflower oil	400ml/14fl oz coconut milk
4 shallots, sliced	2 tbsp finely chopped fresh coriander,
2 garlic cloves, crushed	to garnish
2 fresh red chillies, very finely chopped	lime wedges, to serve
1 fresh green chilli, seeded and chopped	
2.5cm/1in piece root ginger, grated	FOR THE STOCK
2 tsp ground coriander	2 bay leaves
1 stalk lemon grass, finely chopped	1 stalk lemon grass, crushed
2 tsp turmeric	3 kaffir lime leaves
350g/12oz raw tiger or king prawns	6 black peppercorns
in their shells	1 onion, halved
115g/4oz beansprouts	

Put the chicken in a pan with enough water to cover and add the stock ingredients. Bring to the boil and simmer gently for about 1 hour or until the chicken is cooked through. Remove from the heat and leave to cool in the stock.

When the chicken is cool enough to handle, remove it from the pan and cut all the meat from the carcass; set the meat aside. Discard the skin and return the bones and carcass to the stock. Bring to the boil and boil to reduce to 1 litre/1 3/4 pints. Strain the stock and set aside.

Heat the oil in a wok or large open frying pan. Add the shallots, garlic, red and green chillies, ginger, ground coriander, lemon grass and turmeric. Stir-fry for 1–2 minutes or until the shallots soften. Add the strained chicken stock and the prawns and bring to the boil.

Meanwhile, cut the chicken meat into 2.5cm/1in strips, and divide among the serving bowls, along with the beansprouts. Keep warm.

Add the noodles and coconut milk to the wok and simmer for 2 minutes or until the noodles are cooked. Ladle the hot noodle broth over the chicken and beansprouts. Garnish with the chopped coriander and serve, accompanied by lime wedges.

SEARED TUNA ON JAPANESE-STYLE NOODLES

For best results and flavour, use fresh tuna, rather than tuna that has been frozen. To keep the shape of the tuna while it is cooking, use it straight from the refrigerator. This dish looks most attractive when served in a bamboo steamer basket.

225g/8oz thin soba noodles	freshly ground black pepper
2 tsp sesame oil	2 spring onions, finely chopped
1 tbsp mirin	
350g/12oz piece of tuna,	TO SERVE
2cm/³/4 in thick	shredded pickled ginger
	soy sauce

Cook the noodles in plenty of boiling water for about 4 minutes or according to packet instructions. Drain and toss with half of the sesame oil. Keep warm while you cook the tuna.

Heat a heavy frying pan over a high heat. The pan is hot enough if you can hold your hand over it for no more than 5 seconds. Combine the mirin and the remaining sesame oil in a small bowl and brush over both sides of the tuna.

Place the tuna in the hot pan and press down with a spatula. Cook for 1 minute. Turn and cook on the other side for 1 minute. The tuna will now be pink in the middle and well done on the edge. If you prefer, the tuna can be cooked for slightly longer. Remove from the pan, cover and leave to rest for 1 minute.

Grind some black pepper over the tuna and put it on a carving board. Holding the fish in shape with one hand, slice it thinly with a very sharp knife.

Place the noodles on a serving platter, and arrange the tuna slices on top. Sprinkle the tuna with the spring onions and serve accompanied by shredded pickled ginger and soy sauce.

SQUID WITH CHILLI AND GARLIC

The texture of squid makes it very satisfying to eat. Take care not to overcook – the dish should taste zingy and fresh.

20 small squid, tentacles discarded	1 tbsp soy sauce
115g/4oz rice vermicelli noodles	1 tbsp mirin
1 tbsp sunflower oil	2 tbsp black bean sauce
1 tsp sesame oil	pinch of sugar
2 tbsp grated root ginger	2 tbsp chopped fresh coriander
1 fresh green chilli, chopped	salt and freshly ground black pepper
2–3 garlic cloves, crushed	lemon wedges, to serve

Cut the tapered end off each squid tube, and cut open down one side. Open out flat to form a square. Using a sharp knife, score a criss-cross pattern on the inside of the squid. Set aside.

Cover the noodles with boiling water and leave to stand for 3–5 minutes or according to packet instructions. Drain and keep warm.

Put the sunflower oil, sesame oil, ginger, chilli and garlic into a wok or large open pan, and cook over a moderate heat until the mixture is fragrant. Add the squid and stir-fry for about 5 minutes or until cooked. Remove the squid and keep warm.

Add the soy sauce, mirin, black bean sauce and sugar to the wok and boil for 2 minutes. Add the coriander; taste and adjust the seasoning.

Spoon the squid and sauce over the noodles and serve piping hot, garnished with lemon wedges.

Above: Teriyaki Salmon with Noodles

MEAT NOODLES

Many of the cuisines of Asia have developed clever and delicious ways to make a small amount of meat go a long way, particularly in recipes using noodles. With the addition of vegetables such as peppers or beansprouts, a satisfying and nutritious meal can be made in next to no time. All recipes serve 4–6.

MONGOLIAN HOT POT

This is a fondue-type dish, cooked at the table. The traditional cooking vessel, sometimes known as a Peking hot pot, is a round metal dish with a funnel in the centre. Hot charcoal is put into the funnel to keep the stock simmering. An electric wok or a large fondue pot are more modern alternatives.

400g/14oz Chinese flat wheat noodles	4 spring onions, cut into 2.5cm/1in pieces
200g/7oz Chinese leaves, shredded	4 slices root ginger
450g/1lb boneless lamb, thinly sliced	1 tbsp soy sauce
2.4 litres/4 pints beef or lamb stock	1 bay leaf

FOR DIPPING SAUCE 1
120ml/4fl oz soy sauce
1 spring onion, finely chopped
1 garlic clove, crushed
1 tbsp sunflower oil

FOR DIPPING SAUCE 2
6 tbsp wine vinegar
2.5cm/1in piece root ginger, finely chopped
1 tsp shredded pickled ginger

FOR DIPPING SAUCE 3
6 tbsp peanut butter
2 tbsp sesame oil
2 tbsp water

1 tbsp soy sauce
1 tbsp chilli sauce

First make the dipping sauces. Mix together the ingredients for each sauce, and transfer to serving bowls.

Cook the noodles in boiling water for 2 minutes, just to blanch. Drain and arrange on a platter with the Chinese leaves. Arrange the thinly sliced lamb on another platter.

Bring most of the stock to a simmer and pour into the hot pot, wok or fondue pot. Add the spring onions, ginger, soy sauce and bay leaf. Return to a simmer.

Each person uses chopsticks or a fondue fork to take pieces of lamb and cook them in the simmering stock for about 30 seconds, then dips the lamb into one of the dipping sauces before eating.

After the stock has been flavoured by the lamb, the noodles and Chinese leaves are either dipped and cooked by each person, or added to the hot pot with any remaining stock and cooked together to make a tasty soup.

RED BEEF NOODLES

For any cook wanting to experiment with Asian cuisine, a spice grinder is a great time-saver instead of the traditional pestle and mortar.

4 red peppers, halved, seeded and cored	450g/1lb sirloin steak, cut into strips
600g/1¼lb fresh udon noodles	1cm/⅜in wide
1 tbsp sunflower oil	fresh red basil leaves, to garnish
2 tsp yellow mustard seeds	

FOR THE SPICE PASTE

1 tbsp coriander seeds	2 tsp sesame oil
2 garlic cloves, crushed	2 tbsp tomato purée
5cm/2in piece root ginger, shredded	2 tsp rice vinegar
1 tbsp caster sugar	1 tsp cayenne pepper
1 tbsp soy sauce	2 tbsp sesame seeds

First make the spice paste. Grind the coriander seeds, garlic and ginger together in a mortar and pestle or spice grinder. Add the sugar, soy sauce, sesame oil, tomato purée, rice vinegar, cayenne and sesame seeds. Set aside to infuse.

Preheat the oven to 180°C/350°F/Gas 4. Roast the peppers for 30 minutes or until the skin has blistered (alternatively, grill under a medium-high grill for 15 minutes). Put into a plastic bag, or cover with damp kitchen paper, and leave until cool enough to handle. Peel off and discard the skin and finely chop the flesh.

Cook the noodles in plenty of boiling water for 2 minutes or according to packet instructions. Drain.

Heat the oil in a wok or large open pan over a moderate heat. Add the mustard seeds and cover the pan immediately. The seeds will pop in the hot oil; when the popping has subsided, remove the lid.

Add the spice paste and stir-fry until it is fragrant. Increase the heat, add the chopped red pepper and stir-fry for 1 minute, then add the strips of beef. Stir-fry over a high heat for 2 minutes or until the beef is just cooked. Spoon the mixture over the noodles, garnish with red basil leaves and serve immediately.

PORK BALLS

An Oriental version of spaghetti and meatballs, in a sweet-sour sauce.

450g/1lb minced pork	4 tbsp caster sugar
1 tbsp dry sherry	6 tbsp garlic vinegar
1 tsp salt	6 tbsp tomato purée
1 egg, lightly beaten	6 tbsp orange juice
3 spring onions, finely chopped	225g/8oz pineapple, fresh or canned in
1 tsp ground coriander	natural juice, finely chopped
1 tsp ground star anise	300ml/10fl oz chicken stock
1 tsp grated root ginger	225g/8oz egg thread noodles
3 tbsp soy sauce	lemon wedges, to garnish

In a large bowl combine the pork, sherry, salt, egg, spring onions, coriander, star anise and ginger. Shape the mixture into 12 or more balls and place on a tray. Chill for at least 20 minutes.

In a pan large enough to hold all of the pork balls, mix together the soy sauce, sugar, vinegar, tomato purée, orange juice, pineapple and stock. Bring to a gentle boil. Add the pork balls and simmer for 15 minutes or until the balls are cooked through.

Meanwhile, pour boiling water over the noodles and leave to stand for 3 minutes or according to packet instructions. Drain and keep warm.

Divide the noodles among the serving plates and spoon the pork balls and sauce over them. Serve hot, garnished with lemon wedges.

MISO RAMEN

In this healthy Japanese dish, a small quantity of beef is made to go a long way by being sliced very thinly.

1 piece of konbu, about 7.5cm/3in square	salt and freshly ground black pepper
50g/1½oz French beans, halved	1 tbsp sunflower oil
300g/10oz ramen noodles	200g/7oz topside beef, thinly sliced across
1 litre/1¾ pints strong beef stock	the grain
3 tbsp miso paste	50g/1½oz watercress
2 tsp sesame oil	2 spring onions, finely sliced
1 tbsp mirin	1 tbsp shredded pickled ginger
chilli flakes to taste	wasabi paste, to serve

Soak the konbu for 15 minutes in warm water to cover. Drain and shred finely. Blanch the beans in boiling water for 1 minute. Refresh and drain. Set aside.

Pour boiling water over the noodles and leave to stand for 2 minutes or according to packet instructions. Drain.

Heat the stock without boiling and stir in the miso, sesame oil, mirin, konbu and chilli flakes to taste. Season well. Bring to a gentle simmer.

Heat the sunflower oil in a wok or large open pan over a high heat and stir-fry the beef and beans for 1 minute or until the beef is sealed.

Divide the noodles among the serving bowls and ladle the miso stock over them. Top with the stir-fried beef and beans, followed by the watercress, spring onions and shredded pickled ginger. Serve immediately, accompanied by wasabi paste to be added according to personal taste.

CHAR KWEE TAN

The Chinese answer to Singapore Noodles, although this is a richer dish.

225g/8oz flat rice noodles	1 garlic clove, crushed
1 egg	2.5cm/1in piece root ginger, grated
1 tbsp water	1 green pepper, chopped
3 tbsp sunflower oil	180g/6oz peeled raw tiger prawns
1 tbsp yellow bean sauce	200g/7oz canned straw mushrooms, sliced
pinch of salt	50g/1½oz beansprouts
225g/8oz lean boneless pork, cut into	1 tbsp dry sherry
strips about 5 x 2.5cm/2 x 1in	1 tbsp light soy sauce
2 spring onions, cut into 5cm/2in lengths	1 tbsp dark soy sauce

Pour boiling water over the noodles and leave to stand for 5 minutes or according to packet instructions. Drain and cut into 5cm/2in pieces.

Lightly beat the egg with the water. Heat 1 teaspoon of the oil in a wok or large open pan, add the egg and swirl it around to make a very thin omelette. Remove, roll up and leave to cool.

Heat 1 tablespoon of the oil in the wok and add the yellow bean sauce, salt, pork and spring onions. Stir-fry over a high heat until the pork is just cooked, about 3 minutes. Add the noodles and stir-fry for 1 minute. Transfer to a baking dish, cover and keep warm.

Add the remaining oil to the wok together with the garlic, ginger and green pepper. Stir-fry for 1 minute, then add the prawns and stir-fry for another minute or until the prawns turn pink. Add the mushrooms and beansprouts and stir-fry for a further 3 minutes.

Divide the pork noodles among warmed serving plates. Lift the prawns and vegetables from the wok to the noodles, using a slotted spoon. Add the sherry and both soy sauces to the juices in the wok and stir over a high heat until bubbling. Spoon over the noodles and prawns, garnish with strips of omelette, and serve immediately.

BEEF TAO MEIN

A Chinese dish of noodles in a highly flavoured soupy sauce.

1 tbsp sunflower oil	1.2 litres/2 pints beef stock
4 spring onions, sliced	1 tbsp soy sauce
1 garlic clove, crushed	2 tbsp dry sherry
2.5cm/1in piece root ginger, shredded	115g/4oz pak choi, shredded
1 star anise	200g/7oz Chinese flat wheat noodles or
300g/10oz sirloin steak, cut into strips	flat rice noodles
115g/4oz French beans, halved	chilli oil, to serve

Heat the oil in a wok or large open pan. Stir-fry the spring onions, garlic, ginger and star anise over a moderate heat for 1 minute. Add the steak and beans, stock, soy sauce and sherry and bring to a gentle boil. Add the pak choi and simmer for 4 minutes.

Meanwhile, cook the noodles in plenty of boiling water for 4 minutes or according to packet instructions. Drain.

Divide the noodles among the serving bowls and ladle the beef stew over them. Serve immediately, accompanied by chilli oil to be added according to personal taste.

Right: Char Kwee Tan

CHILLI BEEF RAMEN

When making this strongly flavoured ramen stew you can adjust the chilli heat either by altering the quantity or by using milder chillies.

2 fresh green chillies, seeded and chopped	2 shallots, finely sliced
1 tbsp sweet chilli sauce	500g/1lb 2oz ramen noodles
1 tbsp coriander seeds, crushed	1.2 litres/2 pints strong beef stock, hot
2 garlic cloves, crushed	2 tsp chilli flakes
120ml/4fl oz sunflower oil	50g/1¹/₂oz beansprouts
400g/14oz piece of sirloin steak,	4 tbsp fresh coriander leaves
2.5cm/1in thick	1 lime, cut into wedges

In a pestle and mortar or spice grinder, grind together the chillies, chilli sauce, coriander, garlic and 2 tbsp of the oil. Rub this paste all over the beef, pressing well into the flesh. Leave to marinate for up to 1 hour.

Heat the remaining oil in a wok or frying pan and fry the shallots until golden and crisp. Drain on kitchen paper.

Pour boiling water over the noodles and leave to stand for 3 minutes or according to packet instructions. Drain and keep warm.

Heat a wok or large open pan to searing temperature. Put the beef into the wok and press down with a fish slice or spatula. Cook for 2–5 minutes, then turn and cook the other side for 2–5 minutes, pressing down firmly, until done to your liking. Remove the beef from the wok and slice thinly.

Divide the noodles among the serving bowls, ladle the stock over them and top with the beef. Sprinkle over the fried shallots and the chilli flakes. Serve immediately, accompanied by the beansprouts, coriander leaves and lime wedges, which can be added according to taste.

BEEF CHOW MEIN

Chow Mein is many people's first experience of Oriental noodles; it is so delicious it usually makes them want more.

2 tbsp soy sauce	1 tsp sesame oil
5 tbsp hoisin sauce	3 spring onions, sliced diagonally
freshly ground black pepper	2.5cm/1in piece root ginger, shredded
450g/1lb topside beef, thinly sliced	1 red pepper, diced
across the grain	2 tbsp Chinese rice wine or dry sherry
225g/8oz chow mein noodles	120ml/4fl oz strong beef stock
2 tbsp vegetable oil	

Combine the soy sauce and hoisin sauce in a bowl. Season generously with freshly ground pepper. Add the meat strips and leave to marinate for up to 1 hour, but no longer, or the soy sauce will toughen the meat.

Cook the noodles in plenty of boiling water according to packet instructions. Drain and set aside.

Heat both oils in a wok or large open pan over a high heat. Stir-fry the spring onions, ginger and red pepper for 1 minute. Add the meat and the marinade and stir-fry for 2 minutes.

Add the noodles, stir in the rice wine and stock, then mix, using two spoons to lift and stir until the noodles are evenly coated and hot through. Serve immediately.

PORK SOBA

You don't need much pork in this dish, with flavoursome soba noodles and crunchy beansprouts.

1 tsp freshly ground black pepper	100g/3¹/₂oz beansprouts
1 tbsp light soy sauce	2 spring onions, finely sliced
1 tbsp lemon juice	
350g/12oz pork fillet, in one piece	TO GARNISH
300g/10oz soba noodles	2.5cm/1in piece root ginger, shredded
1.2 litres/2 pints strong chicken stock, hot	1 fresh red chilli, sliced

Combine the pepper, soy sauce and lemon juice and spoon over the pork fillet, rubbing well into the flesh. Leave to marinate for 1 hour.

Cook the noodles in plenty of boiling water for 3 minutes or according to packet instructions. Drain and keep warm.

Heat a heavy frying pan. When it is quite hot put in the pork fillet and press down with a spatula. Cover the pan and cook for 4–8 minutes. Turn the pork and cook for 4–8 minutes on the other side, or until cooked to your liking. Remove the pork and leave to rest for 1 minute, then slice thinly.

Ladle the noodles and hot stock into bowls, and add the beansprouts, spring onions and sliced pork. Garnish with ginger and red chilli, and serve immediately.

FILIPINO PORK

The ingredients here may seem unusual, but they work very well. Tomato ketchup is widely used as a flavouring in Asia.

1 can fizzy lime and lemon drink, or	4 boneless pork loin steaks
fizzy lemonade	200g/7oz rice thread noodles
2 tbsp gin	1 tbsp sunflower oil
5 tbsp tomato ketchup	1 fresh green chilli, seeded and finely
2 tsp garlic salt	chopped
1 tbsp Worcestershire sauce	2 spring onions, sliced
salt and freshly ground black pepper	

Combine the lime and lemon drink, gin, tomato ketchup, garlic salt, Worcestershire sauce and seasoning in a large, non-porous dish. Add the pork steaks and turn them in the marinade. Refrigerate for about 2 hours. Remove from the fridge 30 minutes before cooking.

Preheat the oven to 180°C/350°F/Gas 4. Transfer the pork steaks to a roasting tin and roast for 4 minutes. Baste with the pan juices, cover and cook for a further 15 minutes.

Meanwhile, cook the noodles in plenty of boiling water according to packet instructions. Drain and toss with the oil. Stir the green chilli and spring onions through the noodles.

To serve, divide the noodles among the serving plates. Slice the pork steaks into 6 pieces each and arrange on top of the noodles.

Right: Chilli Beef Ramen

VEGETABLES

From a classic Japanese dish of crisp tempura vegetables sitting atop noodles in broth, to Chinese chow mein, to a meat-free version of Thai green curry, here are many ideas to stimulate the palate. Some are substantial vegetarian main meals, others are imaginative side dishes. All recipes serve 4–6.

CHILLI NOODLES

These noodles are just spicy enough for most tastes, and are delicious with a mild curry or any sweet hot dish.

2 shallots	1/2 tsp salt
2 garlic cloves	225g/8oz egg thread noodles
2 small fresh red chillies	2 tbsp sunflower oil
5cm/2in piece root ginger, roughly chopped	1 tbsp water

Put the shallots, garlic, chillies, ginger and salt into a food processor, and blend to a smooth paste.

Pour boiling water over the noodles and leave to stand for 4 minutes or according to packet instructions. Drain.

Heat the oil in a wok and stir in the paste. Stir-fry for 1–2 minutes, until fragrant. Add the water and the noodles, mix with the paste until they are well coated and stir-fry for 3 minutes. Serve immediately.

STIR-FRIED UDON NOODLES

Udon noodles are fantastic stir-fried, making a really satisfying dish that is a meal in itself. If you cannot find fresh noodles, you can use dried; cook them first in boiling water according to packet instructions.

600g/1 1/4lb fresh udon noodles	1 tbsp light soy sauce
3 spring onions, roughly chopped	pinch of sugar
100g/3 1/2oz beansprouts	4 tsp sunflower oil
100g/3 1/2oz shiitake mushrooms, sliced	
1 red pepper, chopped	TO GARNISH
1 garlic clove, crushed	spring onion, finely sliced
2.5cm/1in piece root ginger, grated	Japanese seven-pepper spice or
1 tbsp mirin	lemon pepper
1 tsp chilli oil	pickled ginger or radish

In a large bowl combine the udon noodles, spring onions, beansprouts, shiitake mushrooms and red pepper.

In a small bowl combine the garlic, ginger, mirin, chilli oil, soy sauce, sugar and 1 teaspoon of the sunflower oil.

Heat the remaining oil in a wok or large open pan. When it is very hot, add the noodle mixture and stir-fry over a high heat for 3 minutes. Add the soy mixture and use two spoons to lift and stir so that the noodles and vegetables are coated with the sauce.

Transfer to a heated serving dish, garnish with the spring onion, pepper and pickle, and serve immediately.

INDONESIAN SPICED NOODLES

These highly aromatic noodles are known as Bami Goreng in their native Indonesia.

2 kaffir lime leaves, finely shredded	225g/8oz egg thread noodles
1/2 stalk lemon grass, finely chopped	3 tbsp sunflower oil
3 fresh red chillies, chopped	3 shallots, sliced
2 garlic cloves, roughly chopped	2.5cm/1in piece root ginger, grated
2 cloves	5cm/2in piece galangal, grated
2 tsp coriander seeds	juice of 1 lime
1/2 tsp tamarind pulp, or 2 tsp tamarind	2 tbsp roughly chopped natural peanuts,
juice (page 5)	roasted
2 tsp soft brown sugar	Indonesian soy sauce (kecap manis),
2 tsp turmeric	to serve
1 tsp ground cinnamon	

Grind together the lime leaves, lemon grass, red chillies, garlic, cloves and coriander seeds in a mortar and pestle or spice grinder, to make a paste. Transfer to a small bowl and stir in the tamarind, brown sugar, turmeric and ground cinnamon.

Put the noodles in a large bowl and cover with boiling water. Leave to stand for 3 minutes or according to packet instructions. Drain well.

Heat the oil in a wok or large open pan, add the shallots and cook over a low heat for 10 minutes or until they are soft. Increase the heat, add the ginger and galangal, and stir-fry for 1 minute. Add the spice paste and stir-fry until fragrant.

Add the lime juice and noodles and cook for 4–5 minutes, using two spoons to lift and stir so that the noodles are evenly coated.

Transfer to a serving dish and sprinkle with the peanuts. Serve immediately, accompanied by *kecap manis*.

THAI STIR-FRY NOODLES

A wonderful combination of flavours and textures makes this a very special dish. It looks good too, with spicy noodles and beansprouts rolled up inside a thin omelette and garnished with deep-fried peanuts, tofu and shrimps.

150ml/5fl oz sunflower oil	4 tbsp fish sauce
2 heaped tbsp natural peanuts, sliced	1 tbsp soft brown sugar
2 heaped tbsp diced firm tofu	2 tsp tamarind juice (page 5)
2 tbsp dried shrimps	juice of 1 lime
225g/8oz rice thread noodles	90g/3oz beansprouts
2 dried red chillies, seeded and finely ground	2 eggs
1 shallot, finely chopped	2 tbsp water
1 garlic clove, crushed	3 tbsp chopped fresh coriander

Heat the oil in a wok or large open pan and deep-fry the peanuts until golden brown. Drain on kitchen paper. Deep-fry the tofu and then the dried shrimps. Drain and set aside. Keep the oil in the wok.

Put the noodles in a large bowl and cover with boiling water. Leave to stand for 3 minutes or according to packet instructions. Drain well.

Pour off all but 2 tablespoons of oil from the wok, and add the red chillies, shallot, garlic, fish sauce, brown sugar, tamarind and lime juice. Stir-fry this spice paste until it is fragrant. Add the beansprouts and noodles, and use two spoons to lift and stir the noodles until evenly coated. Transfer to a baking dish, cover and keep warm in a low oven.

Lightly beat the eggs with the water. Pour into the hot wok and swirl around the pan to make a large thin omelette. Turn out on to a plate.

Spread the noodles over the omelette, sprinkle with the coriander and roll it up. Set on a warmed serving plate and garnish with the fried peanuts, tofu and dried shrimps.

CHOW MEIN

In China, this popular dish will vary according to who makes it and which vegetables are in season. Very few Chinese recipes are written down and versions of the same dish vary widely.

4 dried Chinese mushrooms, or fresh shiitake mushrooms	2 tbsp dry sherry
	1 tbsp sunflower oil
400g/14oz chow mein noodles	2 spring onions, sliced
5 tbsp vegetable stock	1 garlic clove, crushed
1 tbsp soy sauce	60g/2oz canned bamboo shoots, drained
1 tbsp oyster sauce	8 canned water chestnuts, sliced
1 tbsp hoisin sauce	115g/4oz beansprouts

If using dried Chinese mushrooms, soak them in warm water for 15 minutes; drain, remove and discard the stalks and slice the caps. If using fresh shiitake mushrooms, slice them. Set aside.

Cook the noodles in plenty of boiling water according to packet instructions. Drain well and set aside.

Combine the vegetable stock, soy sauce, oyster sauce, hoisin sauce and sherry in a bowl and set aside.

Heat the oil in a large wok over a moderately high heat, add the spring onions and garlic and stir-fry for 1 minute. Add the mushrooms, bamboo shoots and water chestnuts and stir-fry over a high heat for 1 minute. Add the beansprouts and sauce mixture and stir until well combined. Simmer for 2 minutes or until the sauce thickens slightly.

Add the noodles to the wok and heat through, using two spoons to lift and stir until the noodles are evenly coated. Serve piping hot.

SPINACH NOODLES

An attractive and appealing combination of broccoli, spinach and egg noodles, with sliced water chestnuts adding an unexpected crunch.

1/2 chicken stock cube	500g/1lb 2oz spinach
225g/8oz medium egg noodles	200g/7oz canned water chestnuts, drained and sliced
180g/6oz broccoli florets	
1 tbsp sunflower oil	salt and freshly ground black pepper

Bring a large pan of water to the boil and crumble in the stock cube. Add the noodles and cook for 4–5 minutes or according to packet instructions. Drain well and set aside.

Blanch the broccoli florets in boiling water; drain well and keep warm.

Heat the oil in a wok or large open pan, add the spinach and stir-fry until wilted, about 5 minutes. Stir in the broccoli florets. Add the water chestnuts and stir-fry for 1 minute. Stir in the noodles and cook, using two spoons to lift and mix until heated through. Season to taste and serve immediately.

YELLOW PEPPER NOODLES

These look stunning! The sweet yellow pepper sauce is the perfect foil for robust soba noodles.

6 yellow peppers
1 whole head of garlic
2 tbsp olive oil
salt and freshly ground black pepper
300g/10oz soba noodles
fresh red basil, to garnish

Preheat the oven to 200°C/400°F/Gas 6. Cut the yellow peppers in half lengthways and remove the seeds and white ribs. Put the pepper halves on a baking tray with the garlic head and bake for 30 minutes. Squeeze the garlic; if it does not yield easily to pressure, return to the oven for a further 20 minutes or so. Put the peppers and garlic into a plastic bag, or cover with damp kitchen paper, and set aside to cool.

When cool enough to handle, peel the peppers and set aside. Cut the top off the garlic to expose the soft cloves. Squeeze the cloves into a food processor or bowl, and blend or mash together with the yellow peppers. Stir in the olive oil and season generously.

Heat the yellow pepper sauce through gently in a small saucepan or in the microwave.

Meanwhile, cook the noodles in plenty of boiling water according to packet instructions. Drain.

To serve, toss the noodles with the sauce and garnish with red basil.

KITSUNE UDON

Tofu, or soya bean curd, has been used in Japan, China and Thailand for centuries. It is an excellent source of protein, and readily absorbs the flavours of other ingredients.

100g/3¹/₂ oz firm tofu
2 litres/3¹/₂ pints dashi broth
4 tbsp dark soy sauce
1 tbsp caster sugar
200g/7oz udon noodles
4 spring onions, thinly sliced diagonally
2 tbsp light soy sauce
1 tsp soft brown sugar
1 tbsp sake or dry sherry
salt
1 tbsp hijiki, soaked in warm water for 10 minutes

Bring a pan of water to the boil, add the tofu, bring back to the boil then drain immediately and cut into small cubes.

Combine 400ml/14fl oz of the dashi broth, 2 tbsp of the dark soy sauce and the caster sugar in a small saucepan. Bring to the boil. Add the tofu cubes and simmer for 5 minutes. Drain, and discard the cooking liquid.

Cook the noodles in plenty of boiling water for 5 minutes or according to packet instructions. Put the spring onions in a small wire sieve and dip briefly into the boiling water; refresh under cold running water and set aside. Drain the noodles, rinse and drain well.

Put the remaining dashi broth and dark soy sauce in a saucepan with the light soy sauce, brown sugar and sake or sherry. Bring to the boil and season to taste with salt.

Arrange the noodles in the serving bowls and top with the tofu, spring onions and soaked hijiki. Ladle in the hot broth and serve immediately.

MUSHROOM NOODLES

You can use any mixture of fresh or dried mushrooms, according to what is available or in season.

2 spring onions
2 tbsp sunflower oil
1 garlic clove, unpeeled, lightly crushed
115g/4oz field or button mushrooms, quartered
60g/2oz shiitake mushrooms, sliced
60g/2oz oyster mushrooms, sliced or halved
15g/¹/₂oz dried porcini, soaked in warm water for 15 minutes
light soy sauce, to taste
225g/8oz egg thread noodles

Cut the spring onions into 5cm/2in lengths and slice each piece lengthways very finely.

Heat the oil with the garlic in a wok or large open pan. Add the spring onions and field mushrooms and stir, then add the shiitake mushrooms followed by the oyster mushrooms. Stir again, then add the porcini. Stir-fry the mushrooms until fragrant. Season with soy sauce.

Put the noodles in a large bowl and cover with boiling water. Leave to stand for 3 minutes or according to packet instructions, then drain.

Pile the noodles on a serving plate. Discard the garlic clove, and spoon the mushrooms and all the pan juices over the noodles. Serve hot.

Above: Yellow Pepper Noodles

GREEN NOODLES

The lovely fresh taste of coriander really comes to the fore in this recipe. You can make the sauce in advance – it will keep for 3–5 days in the refrigerator – and reheat it while you cook the noodles.

1 garlic clove	*2 spring onions, roughly chopped*
1 tsp salt	*1 fresh red chilli, seeded and sliced*
1 tbsp black peppercorns	*3 tbsp lemon juice*
60g/2oz fresh coriander, including stalk	*150ml/5fl oz coconut milk*
and any root	*2 tbsp peanut butter*
2 tbsp chopped fresh parsley, preferably	*225g/8oz flat rice noodles*
flat-leaf	*lemon quarters, to serve*

To make the sauce, grind the garlic, salt, peppercorns and coriander together in a pestle and mortar, blender or spice grinder. Add the parsley, spring onions and chilli and grind to a rough paste.

Transfer the paste to a saucepan and stir in the lemon juice, coconut milk and peanut butter. Bring to a gentle boil, stirring occasionally.

Meanwhile, put the noodles in a large bowl and cover with boiling water. Leave to stand for 5 minutes or according to packet instructions. Drain well.

Toss the noodles with the sauce until they are evenly coated. Serve immediately, with lemon quarters.

DANDAN NOODLES

These are also known as Beggars' Noodles. They make a great meat-free meal, and the nuts give heaps of flavour.

1 tsp chilli oil	*60g/2oz natural peanuts*
1 garlic clove, crushed	*1.5 litres/2¹/2 pints strong chicken stock*
4 tbsp smooth peanut butter	*150g/5oz pickled Chinese cabbage,*
4 tbsp light soy sauce	*roughly chopped*
2 tbsp soft brown sugar	*225g/8oz medium egg noodles*
1 tbsp balsamic or black Chinese vinegar	*2 tsp sesame oil*
2 tbsp sunflower oil	*4 spring onions, finely sliced*
5 dried red chillies	

Combine the chilli oil, garlic, peanut butter, soy sauce, brown sugar and vinegar in a bowl. Whisk well and set aside.

Heat the sunflower oil in a wok or large open pan and fry the chillies until crisp. Drain on kitchen paper. Fry the peanuts in the same oil until golden, and drain on kitchen paper.

Bring the chicken stock to a gentle boil in a saucepan and add half the pickled cabbage. Cover and simmer for 2 minutes only. Keep hot.

Put the noodles in a large bowl and cover with boiling water. Leave to stand for 2 minutes only. Drain well and toss with the sesame oil.

Arrange the noodles in the warmed serving bowls. Whisk the sauce again and spoon over the noodles. Ladle on the hot stock. Serve immediately, accompanied by the spring onions, fried chillies and peanuts and the remaining pickled cabbage, to be added according to personal taste.

THAI SPICED NOODLES

Here we have all the flavours of Thailand in one dish, each complementing the light texture of the noodles.

225g/8oz flat rice noodles	*30g/1oz natural peanuts, roughly chopped*
3 tbsp sunflower oil	*1 tsp soft brown sugar*
1 tsp sesame oil	*60g/2oz fresh chives, cut into short lengths*
¹/2 stalk lemon grass, finely chopped	*5 tbsp lime juice*
2 garlic cloves, sliced	
1 tsp shredded pickled radish	*TO SERVE*
225g/8oz beansprouts	*chopped fresh coriander*
2 tbsp Indonesian soy sauce (kecap manis)	*lime wedges*
2 tbsp fish sauce	*chilli flakes*

Put the noodles in a large bowl and cover with boiling water. Leave to stand for 5 minutes or according to packet instructions. Drain well.

Heat the sunflower oil and sesame oil in a wok. Add the chopped lemon grass and stir-fry over a moderate heat for 2 minutes or until the lemon grass is tender. Add the garlic and pickled radish and stir-fry over a high heat until brown.

Add the noodles and half the beansprouts and mix well. Stir in the soy sauce, fish sauce, peanuts and sugar. Stir-fry over a moderately high heat for 2 minutes, using two spoons to lift and stir until the noodles are evenly coated and heated through. Add the chives, and transfer to a serving plate.

Top with the remaining beansprouts and sprinkle with the lime juice. Serve accompanied by the coriander, lime wedges and chilli flakes, to be added according to personal taste.

Right: Green Noodles

SESAME NOODLES WITH CABBAGE

This noodle dish would be an excellent accompaniment to simply cooked pork or chicken.

200g/7oz egg thread noodles
2 tsp sesame oil
2 tbsp sunflower oil

500g/1lb 2oz Savoy cabbage, finely shredded
1 tbsp soy sauce
3 tbsp toasted sesame seeds

Cook the noodles in plenty of boiling water for 4 minutes or according to packet instructions. Drain well and set aside.

Heat the sesame oil and sunflower oil in a wok or large open pan, add the cabbage and stir-fry for 6–7 minutes or until the cabbage is tender to the bite. Add the soy sauce.

Add the noodles to the wok and stir-fry with the cabbage for about 2 minutes, lifting and mixing with two spoons. Add the sesame seeds, stir and serve immediately.

SICHUAN SPICED NOODLES

The Sichuan province of western China has a very mild climate, and vegetables grow in abundance. Spicy hot and salty flavourings are much used here, and although noodles are not widely eaten in western China, the Sichuan flavourings suit noodles very well.

1 tbsp Sichuan peppercorns
50g/1¹/₂oz root ginger, roughly chopped
3 star anise seeds
¹/₂ tsp ground cinnamon
3 cloves
2 spring onions, finely chopped
1¹/₂ tbsp honey
3 tbsp light soy sauce
1 tbsp dry sherry

1 tbsp sesame oil
1 tbsp sunflower oil
juice of 1 lime
1 tbsp rice vinegar or cider vinegar
pinch of sugar
50g/1¹/₂oz fresh coriander, chopped
225g/8oz medium egg noodles
200g/7oz mustard greens or other Chinese greens

Place the Sichuan peppercorns, ginger, star anise, cinnamon, cloves and spring onions in a blender, pestle and mortar or spice grinder and grind to a rough paste. Transfer to a bowl and add the honey, soy sauce, sherry, sesame oil, sunflower oil, lime juice, vinegar and sugar. Stir in the chopped coriander.

Put the noodles in a large bowl and cover with boiling water to cover. Leave to stand for 5 minutes or according to packet instructions, then drain well.

Heat a wok or large open pan and add the spice paste. Stir-fry until fragrant. Add the noodles and use two spoons to lift and stir the noodles until they are evenly coated in sauce and hot through. Remove to a warmed serving platter.

Stir-fry the greens in the pan juices, and spoon over the noodles. Serve immediately.

STUFFED PEPPERS

Rice vermicelli noodles are great for stuffing vegetables. Here they are mixed with cucumber, coriander seeds and garlic and spooned into baked red pepper halves.

4 red peppers
100g/3¹/₂oz rice vermicelli noodles
¹/₂ cucumber, peeled and chopped
1 tbsp coriander seeds, crushed
1 tbsp sunflower oil

1 tsp sesame oil
2 garlic cloves, crushed
about 1 tbsp soy sauce
2 tbsp sesame seeds, toasted

Preheat the oven to 180°C/350°F/Gas 4. Leaving the stalks on the peppers, cut them in half lengthways and remove the seeds and white ribs. Arrange the pepper halves on a baking tray and cover with foil. Bake for 15 minutes.

While the noodles are still in the packet, break them up into small pieces. Put the noodles in a large bowl and cover with boiling water. Leave to stand for 3 minutes or according to packet instructions, then drain well and set aside.

Mix together the cucumber and coriander seeds.

Heat the sunflower oil and sesame oil in a wok or large open pan, add the garlic and stir-fry for 1 minute over a moderately high heat. Add the cucumber and coriander mixture and stir-fry for about 2 minutes. Add the noodles and use two spoons to lift and toss the noodles until they are coated with the mixture and hot through. Season to taste with the soy sauce.

Put two pepper halves on each serving plate, fill with the noodle mixture and serve hot, garnished with the sesame seeds.

NOODLES ON THE SIDE

A versatile side dish, this is excellent with a curry or any fried dish.

400g/14oz rice noodles, flat or vermicelli
3¹/₂ tbsp lime juice
2 fresh red chillies, seeded and chopped

Cook the noodles in plenty of boiling water, either in a pan or by soaking, according to packet instructions. Drain.

Toss the hot noodles with the lime juice and chopped chilli; serve hot.

LAYERED CRISPY NOODLES

Baked winter vegetables are given an Oriental touch with yellow bean sauce, then sandwiched between deep-fried noodle pancakes.

180g/6oz peeled pumpkin, cubed	30g/1oz butter
1 carrot, cubed	100g/3¹/₂oz egg thread noodles
1 turnip, cubed	3 tbsp yellow bean sauce
1 leek, diced	2 spring onions, finely sliced
1 tbsp sunflower oil	oil for deep-frying
1 garlic clove, crushed	chopped fresh coriander, to garnish
salt and freshly ground black pepper	

Preheat the oven to 180°C/350°F/Gas 4. Mix together the pumpkin, carrot, turnip and leek in a baking dish, and mix in the oil and garlic. Season well and dot with the butter. Cover and bake for 1 hour or until the vegetables are tender.

Meanwhile, put the noodles in a large bowl and cover with boiling water. Leave to stand for 3 minutes or according to packet instructions, then drain well. Divide the noodles into 12 portions and spread each into a flat pancake shape, about 10cm/4in across, on a tray or work surface. Leave to dry completely.

When the vegetables are perfectly tender, reduce the oven heat to very low. Coat the vegetables with the yellow bean sauce and stir in the spring onions. Keep warm in the low oven while you fry the noodles.

Heat 5cm/2in of oil in a wok or large open pan to about 180°C/350°F. Place a noodle pancake on a wire draining spoon and slip it into the oil, being careful to keep its shape. Fry, turning once, until golden brown all over. Drain on kitchen paper and season generously with salt. Fry the remaining noodle pancakes in the same way.

To serve, sandwich the vegetable mixture between pairs of fried noodle pancakes and sprinkle liberally with coriander.

LEMON AND PARSLEY NOODLES

This flavouring is based on the Mediterranean gremolata mixture.

2 tbsp grated lemon zest	salt
2 tbsp finely chopped fresh parsley	noodles of your choice
1 tsp freshly ground black pepper	1 tbsp lemon juice

Combine the lemon zest, parsley, black pepper and salt to taste.

Cook the noodles according to packet instructions. Drain and immediately toss with the lemon juice, followed by the lemon zest mixture. Serve hot.

GREEN CURRIED NOODLES

This is a version of the classic Thai green curry. It can be served without the vegetables if you prefer just a flavoured noodle dish.

225g/8oz flat rice noodles	FOR THE SPICE PASTE
1 tbsp sunflower oil	2.5cm/1in piece galangal, chopped
60g/2oz French beans, blanched	1 tsp coriander seeds
2 courgettes, diced	¹/₂ tsp black peppercorns
250ml/8fl oz coconut milk	3 cloves
115g/4oz Thai spinach, or ordinary	1 stalk lemon grass, roughly chopped
spinach	4 tbsp chopped fresh coriander
juice of 1 lime	3 garlic cloves
2 tbsp shredded fresh basil	2 shallots, chopped
1 tbsp chopped fresh coriander	6 fresh green chillies, seeded
1 tbsp chopped fresh mint	1 tsp shrimp paste
	2 kaffir lime leaves

To make the spice paste, grind all the ingredients together in a large mortar and pestle or spice grinder. Set aside.

Put the noodles in a large bowl, cover with boiling water and leave to stand for 3 minutes or according to packet instructions. Drain well.

Heat the oil in a wok and add the spice paste. Stir-fry until fragrant. Add the beans and courgettes and stir-fry over a moderate heat for 1 minute. Add the coconut milk and bring to a gentle boil. Stir in the noodles and spinach. Sprinkle in the lime juice, basil, coriander and mint. Serve immediately.

Above: Green Curried Noodles

Moyashi soba

Although this vegetarian dish is historically misnamed 'soba' by the Japanese, it uses ramen noodles.

5cm/2in piece mooli, finely shredded	1 tbsp mushroom ketchup
2.5cm/1in piece root ginger, shredded	400g/14oz ramen noodles
1 spring onion, finely sliced	180g/6oz firm tofu, cubed
1.5 litres/2¹/₂ pints vegetable stock	60g/2oz watercress
60g/2oz French beans	soy sauce, to serve
1 carrot, cut into matchsticks	

Put the mooli, ginger and spring onion in three small serving bowls.

Bring the stock to the boil in a saucepan and blanch the beans for 2 minutes. Remove with a slotted spoon and set aside. Blanch the carrot matchsticks for 1 minute only, remove with a slotted spoon and set aside. Flavour the stock with the mushroom ketchup.

Cook the noodles in plenty of boiling water according to packet instructions, then drain.

Pile the noodles in the serving bowls. Divide the beans, carrot, tofu cubes and watercress among the bowls. Ladle on the hot stock, and serve immediately, accompanied by the spring onion, ginger, mooli and soy sauce to be added according to personal taste.

Basil noodles with baked tomatoes

For this Californian speciality, a whole handful of fresh basil is used, not just a sprinkling. As a result, the flavour just explodes!

225g/8oz plum tomatoes	30g/1oz fresh basil
1 tsp salt	2 tsp olive oil
1 tsp caster sugar	salt and freshly ground black pepper
225g/8oz egg thread noodles	Parmesan shavings, to serve

Preheat the oven to 180°C/350°F/Gas 4. Halve the tomatoes and toss them with the salt and sugar. Spread them out in a baking tray and bake for about 1 hour or until they have collapsed. Leave to cool.

Cook the noodles in boiling water for 3–4 minutes or according to packet instructions. Drain well and keep warm.

Put the basil in a blender or food processor and blend in enough olive oil to make a paste. Add this to the noodles and stir until they are evenly coated. Season generously with black pepper and salt to taste.

Spoon the tomatoes over the noodles. Sprinkle with Parmesan shavings, and serve.

Tempura soba

The ultimate in contrasts: soba noodles in broth topped with tempura – deep-fried vegetables in a crisp, light batter. A dipping sauce is served alongside, for the tempura.

1 carrot, cut into strips about	115g/4oz sweet potato, cut into
1 x 4cm/³/₈ x 1¹/₄in	2cm/³/₄in dice
60g/2oz broccoli florets	oil for deep-frying
60g/2oz French beans	plain flour for coating
1 courgette, cut into strips about	225g/8oz soba noodles
1 x 4cm/³/₈ x 1¹/₄in	1.2 litres/2 pints dashi broth
60g/2oz button mushrooms	

FOR THE DIPPING SAUCE	FOR THE BATTER
5 tbsp mirin	1 egg yolk
5 tbsp soy sauce	450ml/15fl oz ice-cold water
3 tbsp dried bonito flakes	180g/6oz plain flour
	pinch of bicarbonate of soda

First make the dipping sauce. Bring the mirin to the boil in a small saucepan and boil to reduce by half. Stir in the soy sauce and bonito flakes, and return to the boil. Immediately remove from the heat and strain. Transfer the sauce to a serving dish and set aside.

Blanch the carrot strips in boiling water for 1 minute, refresh under cold running water and drain well.

Prepare all the remaining vegetables, then make the batter. Stir the egg yolk with the cold water. Sift in the flour and bicarbonate of soda and stir until smooth.

Heat oil in a wok or deep fat fryer to 180°C/350°F. Coat the vegetables lightly in flour. Working in batches, dip them into the batter and then immediately deep-fry in the hot oil for about 1 minute. Drain on kitchen paper and keep warm.

Cook the noodles in the boiling dashi broth for 4 minutes or according to packet instructions. Drain, reserving the broth.

Pile the noodles into the serving bowls and ladle in the broth. Top each bowl with a few deep-fried vegetables. Serve immediately, accompanied by the dipping sauce for the vegetables.

RECIPE INDEX

First published in 1996 by

George Weidenfeld & Nicolson Limited

The Orion Publishing Group

Orion House

5 Upper St. Martin's Lane

London WC2H 9EA

British Library Cataloguing-in-Publication Data
A catalogue record for this book is available
from the British Library.

ISBN 0-297-83581-5

Designed by The Design Revolution, Brighton

Editor: Laura Washburn
Stylist: Roisin Nield
Home Economist: Cara Hobday